Camera Obscura
Into the Dark Room of Faith

John McCulloch

Charleston, SC
CreativeSpace 2016

For now we see in a mirror, dimly, but then we will see face to face. Now I know only in part; then I will know fully, even as I have been fully known. And now faith, hope, and love abide, these three; and the greatest of these is love. (1 Corinthians 13:12-13)[1]

---

[1] All Bible quotations will be taken from the *New Revised Standard Version* (Oxford: Oxford U.P., 1995).

For Tom and Annette. It was those conversations on the 28th floor of the Red Road Flats that led me to writing this book.

Table of Contents

Introduction

Camera Obscura: God in Our Image

Oh night thou was my guide
Oh night more loving than the rising sun
Oh night that joined the lover to the beloved one
transforming each of them into the other.

St John of the Cross, *Dark Night of the Soul* (variant adapted for music by Loreena McKennitt).

This book is about my journey of faith. A journey which has oscillated between certainty and conviction in my youth, to growing doubts and uncertainties in later years. Through the topsy-turvy circumstances of life, I have found myself questioning the view of God I was brought up with. These questions have stemmed from different places: the suffering in our world, the problematic nature of certain 'terror' passages in the Bible, the interface of faith with science and philosophy, the changing role of religion in our society.

In the following chapters I reflect on all of these issues. I do not claim to have found all the answers, as faith is ultimately a mystery which we must embrace and live by, even when we cannot fully make sense of it with our rational minds. If we could ever fully understand or domesticate it, it would no longer be faith. Faith calls us deeper than what our limited minds can process. Faith does not grow in absence of doubt and questions, but through them.

Every time we come to God in prayer, opening ourselves up for the possibility of divine love to transform us, constitutes an act of worship....At the end of the day, the reason why I am a Christian and still have faith, is because

Introduction

I am convinced of the transforming power of love. God is love, and when human beings are moving in love, our world is changed. The miracle of seeing how the human heart can change from hardness and violence to love, is one of the greatest miracles of all.

I know that the reason why I am a Christian is not because of rational explanations, historical reasons (as important as these may be) or any other kind of human endeavour; it is because I have experienced the love of God first hand, and seen its power to transform lives and our world.

But I have found, like St John of the Cross that faith is often lived out in the midst of darkness, where we cannot clearly see the way ahead. The reference to 'the dark room of faith' is not meant to be negative, although I realise that many will initially read it as such. The darkness, as St John of the Cross says in his devotional poem can become 'more loving than the rising sun', because it is a place where we face our vulnerability and loneliness, without all the answers to our questions, without being able to see very far, and it is there where God can meet us.

True faith is not tested when everything is going well, and when we can see the road ahead. It is tested and tried in the depths of night, where doubts and fears abound. And it is there where we too can be transformed by the love of God. The darkness need not be a place of fear, but a place where we encounter our beloved, who longs to make us whole by transforming us through love.

'Camera Obscura' means 'dark chamber' in Latin. It was a wooden box with a hole in it for light to enter, and an image could be rotated and projected upwards and then traced. Its basic principles were used to make the first cameras.

Introduction

The reason why I have chosen it for the title of this book is three-fold: firstly, it shows how beautiful images can emerge from the dark chamber, which ties in with the poem of St John of the Cross. Secondly, it acts as a corollary to the apostle Paul's view of faith and awareness that 'we see through a glass darkly', and 'only in part'; we do not have the full picture, and this should keep us humble and open to other viewpoints. The third reason is the French semiotician Roland Barthes. In 1980 he wrote a deeply personal reflection on the death of his mother. The title of the book was *Camera Lucida: Reflections on Photography*. It is a profound meditation on death, loss, spectres and the power of photography to evoke memories. Barthes looks at the way in which we process images, and how both the context of images and the viewer, conditions how we process that image. 'Camera lucida' is also an optical device which was used to help artists and architects draw, but as its name suggests, functioned by light being reflected into a surface. Unlike the Camera Obscura it did not project an image.

In our modern day world of digital photography and selfies, we can often forget how photography once was developed. As a child I remember my father taking the camera film and leaving it to soak in a dark room. If any bright light entered, the picture would be ruined. Great care was taken to only expose the film to the dimmest of light, and little by little, the image would be revealed.

For me, this is a picture of faith. Something that is forged in the dark...but if we have the patience to wait and open our hearts to God's love, then we too can be gradually transformed, bearing the very image of Christ, which is what our world so badly needs.

Unlike Barthes, I will not be using photographic images to reflect on in this book. Instead I will be referring to the images we have and project of God in our minds, and in the Bible. What is it that we are saying, when we claim that something is done 'in the name of God'? Philosopher and theologian John Caputo has done more work than most in this area, by questioning what lies 'under the name' of God. I am indebted to his work and will be referencing it throughout.

But anyone reading this book as pure theology or philosophy will be disappointed. My background is in literature, and for much of my academic life I lectured in Spanish literature. Although I have always read and engaged with philosophy and theology, it is only recently that I have started to think through the cross-over of all three.

This book very much combines these different interests, which are read through the prism of my own experience. I do not claim authority in any of the areas I discuss, and may be wrong on many issues. For those readers who are still with me, what you will read is a work in progress, where my wrestling with faith is exposed and taken to extremes. I know that it may offend both my atheist and conservative Christian friends alike. But I firmly believe that we are called to love each other despite our differences.

In any case, to duck the issues would be dishonest. And my hope is that other readers who may have experienced similar questions, may find some degree of comfort.

I do not claim to have it all figured out. Quite the contrary. My interpretation of scripture is only one view. If I close down all other readings and fossilise my own, it risks becoming one more fundamentalist reading. And or our world certainly does not need this.

In the chapters that follow, I attempt to open up scripture to explore its richness and vitality, its openness and possibility, and the power of its narratives to speak into our lives and our world.

Chapter 1

Young Earth God

In the beginning when God created the heavens and the earth, the earth was a formless void and darkness covered the face of the deep, while a wind from God swept over the face of the waters. (Genesis 1:1-2)[2]

Introduction

I was brought up in a conservative Christian context where we were taught to believe the Genesis creation story literally. Charles Darwin, Aldous Huxley and other brilliant scientists and intellectuals were demonised and denounced for presenting ideas that 'contradicted' the teachings of the Bible. The Bible was revered as an 'authoritative' book, which did not need to answer to advances in science, philosophy or anthropology, but floated above reality in a Platonic stratosphere of its own. Verses and passages were often plucked out of their original context, and used to affirm or deny certain points of view. Questioning and challenging the Biblical text was a sign of a humanistic mind set, which needed to be purged. After all, it was questioning God in the Garden of Eden that had brought about 'the fall' and had opened the doors to the reign of sin and death. Talking serpents did not just belong to the domain of *The Jungle Book* it seemed, but apparently had existed before Walt Disney immortalised them. The world was presented in black and white terms. A battle between good and evil, right and wrong, certainty and doubt.

How had this come about? How did a collection of texts, written and re-edited down the ages, translated and re-interpreted into different linguistic communities, grouped together and canonised by human decisions

---

[2] All quotations from The Bible will use the New Revised Standard Version (NRSV).

deciding what to include and what to leave out, end up being read through the straight-jacket of literalism?. It wasn't until much later that I began to question what I had been taught as a child. This isn't to say that I threw out the baby with the bath water of my childhood beliefs, as there were many valuable truths about life and the human condition which grew like wild flowers amongst the concrete slab-stones of literalism; but it wasn't until those concrete structures began to crack, that I began to realise that God was far bigger, far greater, and far more inspiring than the one who was imprisoned within the straight-jacket of my literalist imagination.

Texts and Contexts

The philosopher and literary critic Jacques Derrida argues that all texts deconstruct themselves. What he means by this is that when we pay close attention to the context in which a particular text was written, whilst at the same time remaining critical about the presuppositions we bring to a particular text, the meaning of the text is problematised. Language evolves and changes over time, as do systems of belief. All of this affects the way in which we interpret texts. Literalism adopts a surface reading of the text and closes off all other possibilities. Derrida's project consisted in allowing a break away from established confines and encourage multiple meanings and alternative readings to emerge.

Let us consider a simple example by looking at the phrase 'God is love', taken from 1 John 4:8. Upon an initial reading most would say that this is a pretty clear statement. However, when we ask questions about the words, it emerges that this verse can be read very differently depending on your theological outlook. For some, because God is love he must deal out eternal retribution for sin and evil, so the creation of hell is a direct result of his love. Love and punishment need to be understood together. However, for another Christian reading this verse, it is precisely because God is love that the idea of eternal torment is seen as contradictory, barbaric and nonsensical.

The same phrase can lead to radically different conclusions, because language deconstructs, it is an open system rather than a closed one. Deconstructive readings open up the possibilities of the text, and guard against locked-down and restrictive interpretations. Deconstruction recognises the role the reader plays in shaping a text's meaning, because there is no such thing as a 'pure' text as such, because we always approach texts within the framework of our particular interpretive mechanism.

Furthermore, the Bible itself resists readings that lock it down, as different passages question other ones. It evolves and changes depending on context and the set of circumstances which reflect the author(s) times. Ultimately, it resists all attempts to reductively homogenise it through the mince-maker of literalism.

Of course, most of us now recognise that this way of reading the Biblical text(s) is a relatively recent approach. The rabbinical tradition and early Judaism would have warned against purely literalist readings of the holy texts. God was revered as the one who could not be contained or domesticated, and all that language can do is offer a space for both God and humankind to communicate. But the written word was not to be understood as a straight-jacket, but as living and breathing with a dynamism when engaged in a context of worship. The words of the holy texts were to be wrestled with. Karen Armstrong argues that:

The recent preoccupation with Scripture is the result of a widespread religious revival, but also represents a literalistic approach to the sacred texts that would once have been regarded as exceedingly simple-minded. People trained in the rational ethos of modernity expect truth to be logical and accurate. If these sacred texts are not scientifically or historically sound, many assume that they cannot be true at all. But in the past the faithful immersed themselves in their holy books for an experience that went beyond mundane reality and could not be apprehended by ordinary, secular modes of thought.[3]

Armstrong not only reminds us of the contexts in which the sacred texts were written and edited, but the importance of considering how these texts were approached by the communities of faith who engaged with them:

Anyone who simply read the Bible literally 'as a book presenting narratives and everyday matters', had missed the point. There was nothing special about the literal Torah: anybody could write a better book—even the Gentiles had produced greater works.[4]

Whilst Armstrong is possibly taking the argument too far here, she is right to highlight the important issue of how communities of faith engage with the reading process. She reminds us that the ancient 'midrash' (interpretation) had to be 'guided by the principle of compassion'.

---

[3] Karen Armstrong, 'The Idea of a Sacred Text', in *Sacred: Books of the Three Faiths: Judaism, Christianity, Islam*, edited by John Reeve. Essays by Karen Armstrong, Everett Fox, F.E. Peters. Catalogue contributions by Colin. F.Baker, Kathleen Doyle, Scot McKendrick, Drew Nersessian and Llana Tahan (London: The British Library, 2007), 14-20 (p.14).
[4] Karen Armstrong, *The Bible: The Biography* (London: Atlantic Books, 2007), 151.

She points out that 'At the end of his exegesis, Hillel uttered a *miqra*, a call to action: "go study!"'. When they studied the Torah, rabbis should attempt to reveal the core of compassion that lay at the heart of all legislation narratives in the scriptures—even if this meant twisting the original meaning of the text'.[5]

The way in which I had been brought up to read the Bible was a relatively modern development fuelled by the invention of the printing press around the 15th century. In fact, what is ironic is that the confidence in the Bible to 'shine truth' on particular situations and which gave the Bible its 'authority' to challenge scientific and philosophical thought, was largely brought about by the 17th century Enlightenment project.

With the advent of the printing press the written word was circulated and made available to a much wider range of society to those who had access to hand-copied versions of texts. The scientific revolution coincided with the Age of Enlightenment, and a new emphasis on rationalism began to replace what was perceived as medieval obscurantism. Of course, any attempt to draw neat lines between different epochs is doomed to failure, as ideas evolve gradually through the historical process.

Linking literalism with The Age of Enlightenment would probably alarm most 'Bible believing Christians' (and I will engage with what is meant by this statement further on), as they would almost certainly see the Enlightenment as a humanistic endeavour which detracted from the power of religion and the church. The Enlightenment project brought about the great age of the Encyclopaedia, fuelled by a desire to move away from medieval superstition and aided by the technological

[5] Armstrong, *The Bible*, 82, 3.

break-through in mass printing. The world was documented, studied and 'textualised' in ways that had been impossible before. The written text had authority. The world was brought under the light of rational, scientific inquiry, and anything that did not fit into this world view was discarded as coming from a medieval superstitious mind-set which our enlightened world had outgrown. Scientific certainty was building a rapidly modernising world, enshrining progress and an unrelenting march forward into a stage in history dominated by the emergence of civil democratic society. This is our cultural heritage in the West. The prioritisation of the written word over oral accounts was almost set in stone.

This is, of course, an over-simplification of a much more complex set of circumstances, but there is little doubt that the 'literalist' approach to the Biblical texts, in part stems from 17th century European Enlightenment. And what was the justification given to us to approach the Bible this way? That famous passage in 2 Timothy chapter 3 (verses 16,17) which reads 'All Scripture is inspired by God and is useful for teaching, reproof, for correction, and for training in righteousness, so that everyone who belongs to God may be proficient, equipped for every good work'.

Except that this verse could not have been written to prove that the Bible was 'true', given that it was written several hundred years before the Biblical canon had been formed, and was therefore not commenting on the 66 books that we in the Protestant tradition believe to be the Bible. But even if we were to take this verse at face value (not that this is ever possible, for we can never approach a text neutrally, but always bring our particular interpretive frameworks to bear on the reading process), note that it says 'Inspired by God' (or 'God breathed' in other versions). It doesn't say 'dictated by God', which is what many

Muslims believe about the Qur'an. It says God inspired/breathed. The word in the Greek original for 'God breathed' is a compound word made up of 'Theos' and 'pneuma' (*Theopneustos*), meaning God and Spirit. The image is one of divine creativity, permeating everything, like the Spirit hovering over the deep in the first chapter of Genesis, bringing created order out of formlessness. It is a word combination that implies movement, adaptability, life. It is a very different concept to that of dictated word. Dictation implies something which is set in stone. The very words uttered by the speaker are written down by the listener.

When I was at school in Spain as a child, not long after Spain had transitioned to democracy, one of the exercises in our language class was dictation. The teacher would dictate a passage of literature, and we would be assessed on how accurately we wrote it down. We would write down verbatim what we had heard, and would be marked in the accuracy of our writing.

But this is not the way in which the Biblical texts were written. The word 'breathe' infers something which is alive. Something that is essential to living organisms. It is the same verb that is present in the Genesis creation text when God breathes life into humankind. It is the opposite of the intractable straight-jacket metaphor, but is shaped by whatever it breathes into. Breathing cannot be understood apart from an organism or body. In this sense it is deeply incarnational. It emerges through a living organism, rather than being imposed from above. It allows for mystery and wonder, which break out of the narrow dictates (note that this is where we get the word dictator from) which reduce God to particular narrow interpretation of a written text.

How we Read

Before we go any further, let me nail my colours to the mast, to avoid any confusion. I believe that the Bible is inspired, and different to other works of history and literature. It is literature, but it is more than literature. There is no question in my mind that it is one of the ways in which God speaks to us. The other means are the natural world, the witness of the Church and community of faith, subjectively and individually (existentially), and through the process of history and evolving scientific/cultural contexts in which we live. I do not limit God's revelation to Scripture, because it cannot be contained by words. I think Scripture has a high role and value, because it is a record of how we have understood God through the ages, with all of our misconceptions and blind spots along the way, in addition to moments of real transcendence and epiphany. The Bible is different to other great literature such as Shakespeare, Dante and Cervantes, because, as Karen Armstrong has argued, it emerged and was forged in the context of faith-seeking communities, in a context of worship, and it is one of the ways in which God communicates. It has authority. The Bible also reveals and shows us Jesus Christ. I have a high view of Scripture and of its intrinsic authority, which is why I cannot settle for literalistic reductionism.

When we, both as individuals and as communities, open ourselves up to the possibility of the divine, of transcendence, something happens. The boundaries of our individual selfhood are expanded. A space opens up, a sacred space, where God can come. But God does not come in manageable bite sized pieces. She[6] is not domesticated

---

[6] Because God is spirit, God cannot be gendered. We have gendered God down the centuries from within the patriarchal structures which have dominated human history until the advent of the 20th century. I will therefore refer to God sometimes as 'He' and sometimes as 'She' to remind us of this.

or easily tamed, but is mystery, beyond the grasp of our human intellect and reasoning.

In my conservative upbringing there wasn't much room for mystery. Instead, God had spoken clearly in The Bible. Our duty was to just read it as it was presented to us, and act accordingly. This was the mind-set with which we were taught to read the book of Genesis. This was the prism through which we defended 'creationism' against Darwinian understandings of Evolution through Natural Selection. With this dualistic mind-set Genesis and Darwin could not both be 'true', so Darwin had to be wrong. It never crossed our minds that perhaps Genesis was never written as a factual account. We never thought of considering the first chapters of Genesis within the literary tradition(s) in which it was written. It didn't cross our minds how ancient religious communities would never have measured these texts against a factual and literalist yardstick, but that these texts pointed to something far greater about the human condition, about life and the world; not a literal account of how the world came to be.

I have a lot of sympathy with Richard Dawkins when he alludes to the religious accounts of the world of painting a picture of the origins of life on earth as far less majestic than those presented by science. That is, if we read the sacred texts literally. I have found his scientific writings to be incredibly inspiring and beautiful accounts about the magisterium of science. The demonisation of Dawkins by the Christian Right (especially in the USA but also regrettably in some sectors of UK Christianity as well) is not only profoundly 'un-Christian', but embarrassingly misinformed and misguided. The scientific writings of Dawkins have done more to open up the wonder of the world in which we live, than hundreds of 'creationist' accounts which have been written to discredit Darwinian theories of evolution through Natural Selection. Darwinian accounts of Evolution do not invalidate the Genesis account. Neither does the Genesis account invalidate science. Those interested in delving into this in more detail should read Rabbi Sacks' book *The Great Partnership: God, Science and the Search for Meaning.*[7] Part of what Sacks sets out to do is to argue that science and religion are not to be viewed as mutually exclusive discourses, as many of the new-atheists would have you believe (I am thinking here specifically of figures such as Richard Dawkins, Sam Harris, the late Christopher Hitchens amongst others), but are complementary as they perform different functions. Sacks argues:

> Science is about explanation. Religion is about meaning. Science analyses, religion integrates. Science breaks things down to their component parts. Religion binds people together in their relationships of trust. Science tells us what is. Religion tells us what ought to be. Science describes. Religion beckons, summons, calls. Science sees objects. Religion speaks to us as subjects. Science practices detachment. Religion is the art of attachment, self to self, soul to soul. Science sees the underlying order of the physical world. Religion hears the music beneath the noise. Science is the conquest of ignorance. Religion is the redemption of solitude.[8]

The problem is not with the Biblical text(s) but with our hermeneutical approaches, or put more simply, with the interpretive frameworks which we apply to the texts. Everybody (even the hardened fundamentalist) would agree that we approach texts differently, depending on their particular genres. For example, you would approach Albert Einstein's *Theory of General Relativity* very differently to a Shakespearian sonnet or play. One is a scientific treatise, the other is literary. Both contain 'truth'

---

[7] Jonathan Sacks, *The Great Partnership: God, Science and the Search for Meaning* (London: Hodder & Stoughton, 2012).
[8] Sacks, *The Great Partnership*, 6-7.

statements about reality, but do so in different ways. Einstein's will make claims about scientific laws and how light particles travel, whilst Shakespeare's will make claims about the human condition, about love, human emotions and sentiments. To claim that one text is superior to another because of factual truth is to miss the point completely. They are doing different things, and to read them otherwise would be absurd. So why is it that when it comes to the Bible, these kind of distinctions are not made? (I am addressing conservative fundamentalism here, i.e. my past, not the more discerning readers of The Bible).

I would argue that such literalist approaches which claim to uphold and 'believe' the Bible, run the risk of de-valuing its full potential. The very people within the Christian tradition who claim to be 'Bible believing Christians' and defenders of the Bible, can actually domesticate it by closing down possibilities for alternative and complementary interpretations. In fact, most of the time they do not actually read the whole of the Bible in that way in any case, if not they would stone disobedient children, accept arranged marriages of under-aged teenage girls. Women would need to be silent in church, slavery would be defended, the eating of seafood outlawed, in addition to a whole other array of rules and regulations which originated in remote cultures very different to our own. The Bible simply does not lend itself to be read in such reductive terms, and to do so, does it a profound disservice by the very people who claim to be its greatest defenders.

Other Literatures that Influenced Genesis

It is with this in mind, that I would like to offer a different reading of the Genesis account, which is not in confrontation with our understanding of science. Let me say from the start that this reading is not original. Mercifully, there is a rich tradition within Judaism and Christianity which would never read the Genesis account of creation as a scientific literalist account. Instead, they would read the Genesis story as a piece of literature which speaks primarily to the human condition, and which was never meant to rival scientific accounts. In this sense it is inspired, not because of any claims to factual and literal truth, but because it speaks deeply to the human condition. To our developed sense of self-consciousness. To our propensity towards blaming others and not accepting responsibility. To ethical responsibilities which come with freedom. To understanding how my freedom of choice has huge implications for those around me, for good and for bad. To show that we are created in the very image of God. That through us he is creating and re-creating this world. Creation is not a static process which happened and is over and done with, but is ongoing, and we are all invited to be a part of. The book of Genesis reminds us that as human beings we can fall away from the ideals. When we live with only reference to ourselves and not the creator, life-giving God, we often turn to selfishness and self-preservation.

The authors and editors of Genesis were writing in a pre-Copernican and pre-scientific age. It would be several millennia later that Copernicus pointed out that the earth was not the centre of the universe. The writers of Genesis were not writing in a vacuum, but within a world-order where the paradigms of mythical literature informed that particular world view. Genesis is not the oldest account of creation, the Babylonian mythical poem the *Enuma Elish* and the Mesopotamian *Gilgamesh Epic* existed long before the Genesis account was written down. The *Enuma Elish* is widely claimed to have been written between the 18th and 16th century BCE, whilst the Sumerian poetry that informs the Gilgamesh dates from as early as 2100 BCE. The Genesis account however, is now widely understood to have been written around the time of the Babylonian Exile in the 6th century BCE, which would account for the heavy influence of the Babylonian and Summerian mythology it clearly contains.

Even a superficial reading of the *Enuma Elish* reveals striking similarities (and differences) from the early chapters of *Genesis*. The *Enuma Elish* was written on what is known as cuneiform script, which is one of the earliest kind of writing and consists of making marks with a reed on clay tablets. The *Enuma Elish* was written on seven tablets, and consists of 1000 lines. Note that the number seven, like in the Genesis account, is also symbolic in the *Enuma Elish*, and the seven tablets immediately remind us of the seven days of creation in Genesis. Numerous studies have been made comparing the biblical account of creation to that of the *Enuma Elish*, so I will not engage in a detailed comparative analysis here, but will only draw on some of the similarities, before considering the ways in which the Genesis account differentiates from it as well.

Like the Genesis account of creation, the *Enuma Elish* depicts a world made up of expansive waters, when both the sky and the earth were not named, depicting an unformed world. In the *Enuma Elish*, there is a clear differentiation between the sky above and the earth beneath (as in the Genesis account) and presence of chaos, in the form of the female goddess Tiamat.

Here are the opening lines of tablet 1, which will give you a flavour of its lyrical nature and will immediately bring to mind the parallels between it and the Genesis account of creation briefly alluded to above:

When on high the heaven had not been named,
Firm ground below had not been called by name,
When primordial Apsu, their begetter,
And Mummu-Tiamat, she who bore them all,
Their waters mingled as a single body,
No reed hut had sprung forth, no marshland had appeared,
None of the gods had been brought into being,
And none bore a name, and no destinies determined—
Then it was that the gods were formed in the midst of heaven.
Lahmu and Lahamu were brought forth, by name they were called. (10)

Differentiation

What is interesting in my view about Genesis and the *Enuma Elish*, is not just their similarities, but the way in which the authors, editors and redactors of Genesis borrow elements whilst at the same time deliberately differentiate from the *Enuma Elish*. The polytheism of the *Enuma Elish* gives way to monotheism (which makes complete chronological sense in terms of the history of religion, as the early roots of what was to evolve into Judaism differentiated itself from other world religions of the time by embracing a new way of understanding the divine; monotheism). The ancient parent belief systems of Judaism were unique in their journey towards monotheism.

The other main difference between the Genesis account and the *Enuma Elish* is that the latter depicts the creation of the world through a violent struggle between Marduk and Tiamat, as Dominican Priest Timothy Radcliffe has argued:

Young Earth God

Nearly all the myths of their neighbours understood creation as a violent act, the destruction of some monster which embodied the waters of chaos. For example, in the Babylonian epic of creation, the Enuma Elish, Marduk, the storm god, slaughters Tiamat, the goddess of the sea, to make the universe. We can see vestiges of this violent creation in the Old Testament, as when Isaiah looks to the day when 'the Lord with his hard and great strong sword will punish Leviathan the fleeing serpent, Leviathan the twisting serpent, and will slay the dragon that is in the sea' (Isaiah 27:1). But in Genesis, no one gets killed to make the world. The Spirit hovers over the formless void. God speaks a word and everything comes to be.[9]

What makes Genesis unique and deeply life-giving is not that it represents an original, factual, and foundational account of how the world began; rather its inspiration and value are to be found in how it differentiates itself from its sources to portray a God of peace who breathes life over the formless void and brings forth life. As Radcliffe argues above, the absence of violence in the creative act would have been a radical departure from other creation myths around leading up to the time that Genesis was written.

The Genesis account is a picture of how human beings developed what essentially differentiates us from our animal ancestors. Namely, our highly evolved sense of self-consciousness and capacity to reflect on our position in the universe. What separates us from the animal kingdom is our ability to tell stories about ourselves. In fact, our sense of selfhood is profoundly shaped and informed by our own story: i.e. where we come from, where we were brought up, who our parents and siblings are, our memories of the past which shape who we are today, or hopes for tomorrow.

---

[9] Timothy Radcliffe, *Why go to Church: The Drama of the Eucharist* (London & New York: Continuum, 2008), 119.

This heightened ability we have to reflect on ourselves in the universe (self-consciousness) is what makes us human. As human beings we have agency (that is the power to make choices). With choice comes responsibility, because my freedom to choose necessarily has consequences on those around me and for the world, because as humans we live in community with each other, and in 'communion' with the natural world around us.

How we understand 'the fall'

The story of Adam and Eve in the Garden of Eden is a picture of humankind as it evolved towards self-consciousness, and therefore towards ethical accountability. Thus the fig-leaves which they sewed together when they recognised that they were naked represents a highly evolved sense of self-consciousness. An animal has no awareness that it is naked. This is obvious. The recognition of being naked is a human one. With choice comes responsibility, which is illustrated with the picking of fruit from the tree. The so called 'fall' (and it is interesting to note that the word 'fall' does not appear in the Bible) need not be understood as a one-off event which changed the very ecosystem from a state of 'perfection' (whatever that means) to one where sin an evil is present. This is absurd. In fact, it makes little sense even if you read the Genesis account at face value, because the presence of evil is already in the garden in the form of the serpent, so the picture is not one of perfection in any case. Some Christian writers have gone to great lengths to take things back a stage further, and to talk not only about the fall of man as such, but the fall of angels. Michael Lloyd argues that there was 'a prior fall of angels', and goes on to suggest that 'The angelic rebellion actually distorted the whole way in which the material creation developed, luring it away from God's original harmonious purposes, and introducing division, disorder, pain, predation, cruelty, and killing, disease and death'.[10] Lloyd takes as his cue the passage in Isaiah which talks about Lucifer's fall from grace in his attempt to gain equality with God.

But this approach also misses the point of the Genesis story, and lacks any real credibility. Earlier in the same chapter from which I have quoted, Lloyd argues that suffering, death and 'evil' came about through the fall, and were not part of God's plan. I will quote the passage in question in full as it is important to consider the implications of what Lloyd is suggesting:

Evil, suffering and death (at least as we now experience it) have no rightful place in God's good world. They are not part of His original purposes. They are not things that He wants to happen. He did not build them into His World. They occur, not because things have gone the way He wanted, but precisely because they haven't. Suffering is part of the story, not part of the set-up. It is part of the process, but not part of the purpose. It was not intended. It is not intrinsic. It is neither natural nor normal. It is an alien condition which God did not create, but which we have invited into existence.[11]

One of the problems with Lloyd's attempt to deal with the difficult realities of suffering and death is that to claim that suffering is 'not part of the set-up' makes no sense when you consider how ecosystems work. Life on this planet is possible because of ecosystems: organisms feeding off each other, from plankton in the oceans that feed the fish, to mammals on the savannah being eaten by other predators, from lizards that trap and feed on insects. Life is made up of a cycle of birth, growth, death and decay; and that cycle can only function because of

---

[10] Michael Lloyd, *Cafe Theology: Exploring Love, the Universe and Everything* (London: Alpha International, 2005), 82.
[11] Lloyd, *Cafe Theology*, 61-62.

predation. To wilfully assume that all was sweetness and light in the Garden of Eden until the fall, is nonsensical. The very existence of plants and animals could not occur outside of an ecosystem, which by its own very nature is predatory. The Garden of Eden should not be read literally but as ancient mythology and Origin literature, which nonetheless possesses deep truths about our world and the human condition, and inspires us to be good stewards of our natural environment, and responsible in our interactions with our fellow human beings, for all is 'good' and sacred.

Could the view of the 'fall' presented in the Genesis account be understood not so much as a literalist eating of the forbidden fruit, but an insight into the human condition that our actions have consequences, and that as human beings we are faced with situations on a daily basis, and our choices have profound consequences on those around us, for good and for bad? In fact, I would go further and suggest that the Christian idea of 'original sin' (which in itself is contested within the Christian tradition but which I cannot go into now) is very similar to Richard Dawkin's idea of the selfish gene. That is, that in the depths of our very beings as humans, there is the propensity to act selfishly and purely in our own self-interests. Just as Dawkins argues that the fact we have the selfish gene does not justify living that way or organising our societies around that principle, but that being truly human means that we rise above our instincts for the good of all; Christianity also purports that to live selfishly goes against the teachings of God. The importance of the Genesis account is not that disobedience happened once in the Garden, but that as human beings we are confronted with ethical choices on a daily basis, which have consequences for our fellow human beings and the natural environment in which we live. This is what it means to be truly human, to have the freedom to make choices, and the ability to reflect on those choices. When we act selfishly and as if we are the only ones that matter, we fall away from God's ideal. We need to be recreated and restored on a daily basis, to commune with the God who walks in the cool of the garden. The God who is life-giving and love, and who breathes his life into the dust and DNA of our human bodies, so that we are much more than the sum of our physical parts, but we are dignified as human beings charged with the responsibility and gift of living for others. Opening ourselves up to the love of our self-giving God, will lead to us loving our neighbour as ourselves.

If we as a human race loved our neighbour as ourselves, it would change everything. There would be no conflicts, no inter-racial genocide, no exploitation of other's resources, no fear of the other, no violence, no abuse. It would change everything. The world would be the garden depicted in the Genesis story. We would live in communion with our maker and fellow human beings. We would live in harmony and respect of our natural environment.

We are all called to enact this. We are invited to create and re-create this world through self-giving love. To live in this world according to a higher principal than that of human greed and self-preservation, but out of self-giving love like the creator God who gives out of Her love, like a mother birthing a child, who cannot remain in the womb but which must break forth into life; life with all its challenges and complexities. Life with all its choices and possibilities, dangers and suffering. We are called to live life according to the principal of love and giving to others. We are called to use our freedom for the well-being and benefit of others. This is what it means to be truly human. This is why Genesis is inspired. It speaks to the very core of our being as humans on this planet.

Free will and Self-Consciousness

It must be remembered that there is a whole section of philosophical and scientific thought that argues that we are not free as individuals. Biological determinism coalesces with all manner of cultural and philosophical ideas to argue this point. For those interested in one of the best intellectual rebuttals of this, you should read Raymond Tallis' brilliant book *Aping Mankind: Neuromania, Darwinitis and the Misrepresentation of Humanity*[12] (he writes from the position of a committed atheist), in which he re-affirms our humanity from the basis of human freedom of agency. He also militates against reductionist uses of neurobiology and neo-Darwinian genetics which have been used to deny our freedom of choice as human beings. In the opening pages of his introduction he sets out his stall:

[...] I am not a closet creationist. Nor do I seek to promote a supernatural account of humanity. I do not believe that the organism *H. sapiens* came into existence by a separate process from that which gave rise to all other living organisms. Nor is my hostility to a materialist account of consciousness, as expressed in the identification of the mind with brain activity, rooted in a belief in Cartesian dualism, or in the notion that we are immaterial ghosts in the material machine of the mind or the body. I thought I ought to set that straight.

I do not doubt that Darwinism gives an ever more impressively complete account of how the organism *H. sapiens* came into being. But that's not the point: things with us did not stop there. Humans woke up from being organisms to being something quite different: embodied subjects, self-aware in a manner and to a degree not approached by other animals. Out of this, a new kind or realm was gradually formed. This, the human world, is

---

[12] Raymond Tallis, *Aping Mankind: Neuromania, Darwinitis and the Misrepresentation of Humanity* (Durham: Acumen, 2011).

materially rooted in the natural world but is quite different from it.[13]

But let's return to the Genesis story. I have actually met Christians who believe that the natural order of the world changed after the so-called 'fall'. It goes something like this. The world God created in the Garden of Eden was 'perfect'. By this they mean that there was no sin, no evil (even-though the talking serpent was already there). Animals lived together happily (presumably predatory animals like lions and tigers were using their fangs to eat vegetables). Adam and Eve disobeyed by eating of the forbidden fruit, and 'sin' entered the world, changing the natural order from one of peaceful coexistence to one 'red in tooth and claw' as the saying goes.

Anyone who has even the smallest modicum of knowledge about how an ecosystem works, would recognise the folly of this literalist account. As stated earlier, an ecosystem relies on a chain of organisms living off each other for its existence. Even what seems as a peaceful garden is only there because of the cycle of life and death, like that scene out of David Lynch's film *Blue Velvet* which shows a neatly manicured suburban grass lawn, but as the camera gets closer and closer, we are led under the surface of the grass, to a world of predatory insects feeding off each other.

From the tiny amoeba and plankton to plant-life and animals, nothing that exists could exist outside of the circle or birth, growth, death and decay. The idea of a 'perfect' natural world devoid of suffering is just fanciful childlike thinking. Far more coherent a view of the Genesis narrative (which dovetails with what we know from evolutionary biology and genetics) is an account of

---

[13] Tallis, *Aping Mankind*, 11.

humankind attaining the high levels of self-consciousness which makes us different from other animals and hominids. The ability to choose, to exercise freedom of agency, is what it means to be made in the image of God. The 'fall' is the condition we bring about (both individually and corporately because we are social beings) when we act out of selfish desires. When we don't put others' interests above ours. When our thoughts and deeds are carried out to exalt and protect the ego, rather than giving out for the benefits of others, there is a sense in which we 'fall' away from what is ideal. I know that Dawkins explains altruism in evolutionary terms, as those who act altruistically in a group are more likely to survive and pass on their genes, but as a follower of Christ and his teachings, I believe that true human fulfilment is found when we are giving of ourselves to others, and that this cannot be solely reduced to genetics (not that Dawkins does, to be fair to him).

What I am proposing here does not discredit the Biblical text(s). In fact, it is precisely the opposite, as it seeks to do them justice by considering them in the context of their particular generic conventions, and the time in which they were written. God is much bigger than the textual straight-jackets we impose on Her. God is much bigger that our misrepresentations of Her creative love. God ultimately reveals Herself as incarnated in human beings as they respond and open themselves up to that love, like a child who is nurtured by their mother, but who then grows to maturity bearing the marks of that love. God is love. God is pregnant with life-giving potential. God is much more than the illusions we construct. And God's action the world is incarnated through us.

With a heightened sense of selfhood and the ability to reflect on our place in the universe, comes a greater degree of suffering. The degree of suffering for any living being is in direct proportion to their complexity as a biological organism. Let me explain this to avoid misunderstanding. It would be absurd to talk about the suffering of a simple organism such as an amoeba or plankton, for the obvious reason that it lacks the complexity of other living creatures. A conscious animal, by contrast, does suffer considerably: we have all watched nature programmes on the television that depict predatory animals chasing their prey. We have all been moved when witnessing a weaker animal being torn apart as the jaws of the stronger predator lock on the victim. The phrase referring to nature as 'red in tooth and claw' is a familiar one to us all, and one which has caused theologians and philosophers down the years to question the very foundational beliefs of a benign deity who would set in motion a system where there is so much capacity for pain and suffering. The whole theme of theodicy (why a supposedly all-powerful good God can allow suffering) will be considered throughout this book from different angles, although let me lay a disclaimer right away, that far brighter and better informed minds than my own have grappled with this question, and none can really assuage what is essentially in my mind the biggest impediment to faith. Process theology and John Caputo's ideas of a weak God come closest, but not without polemic, as we will see in later chapters.

The times when I have doubted the existence of God (and this has happened increasingly as I get older) have always been related to the issue of theodicy and the fact that we are surrounded by so much pain and suffering in this world.

But let's get back to what we were discussing earlier, namely the different levels of suffering in the animal kingdom. An amoeba has minimal (if any) ability to suffer, whereas as we progress up the evolutionary food chain, the capacity for suffering increases proportionally. A gazelle being mauled by a tiger is obviously undergoing considerable suffering, and will have experienced fear in the build-up to the attack. There is no question about this. However, and this is by no means to be understood as trivialisation of animal suffering or an attempt to not take it seriously, a gazelle's capacity for suffering is less than a human being's, because suffering is intensified considerably the bigger the brain. Let me be clear: what I am not saying here is advocating some horrific form of eugenics, which avers that less intelligent beings suffer less than intelligent ones. That would be both hideous on ethical grounds and downright stupid. What I am suggesting is that our capacity as human beings to reflect on pain (and remember/process pain), which goes hand in hand with our highly evolved sense of self-consciousness which enable us to have memories of pain, both suffered individually but also amongst the families and communities we live in, increases our suffering.

I remember watching a David Attenborough nature programme, where some baby chicklets were being carried away by a fox from under the mother hen's nose (or beak, I should say). I am not diminishing the fact that scenes such as these are incredibly sad to behold, but at the same time I couldn't detach the scene I was watching from the voice-over of the narrator (in addition to the musical score which was specifically composed and edited to shape the emotional impact of the scene) which was talking about the chick's suffering in very humanised and anthropomorphic terms. The mother was depicted as being 'distressed' at the loss of her chicks, the other sibling chicks who are left behind etc. However, given what we know about chick brains, a chick will have no memory of an event such as the one described. It will have no recollection of it. The surviving chicks will have no recollection of the loss of their siblings, not just because their brains cannot compute the world existentially like we do, but because the whole concept of 'sibling' is a human one which we emotively impose on the scene. This may sound like a pretty obvious point to make, but every nature programme I have watched will project human notions of suffering onto the animal context, and in so doing exaggerate the actual suffering of the animals in question. Imagine now for a moment, that we are not dealing with hens and chicks, but with a human mother and her children, some of them killed and others left behind. The level of suffering is on a different scale. The suffering of the surviving siblings will also be intensified. The older siblings who are old enough to carry a memory of the event, to that of a very young or new born child, will affect the way extent and the way in which each suffers, and responds to suffering. Suffering is linked to our evolutionary place in the world's ecosystem.

Chapter 2

Warrior God

The Mind is its own place, and in itself can make a heaven of hell, a hell of heaven. (John Milton, *Paradise Lost*)

When you think of the long and gloomy history of man, you will find more hideous crimes have been committed in the name of obedience than have ever been committed in the name of rebellion. (C.P.Snow)

Language provides the foundation for history, planning, and social control. However, with language come rumors, lies, propaganda, stereotypes, and coercive rules. Our remarkable creative genius leads to great literature, drama, music, science, and inventions like the computer and the Internet. Yet that same creativity can be perverted into inventing torture chambers and torture tactics, into paranoid ideologies and the Nazis' efficient system of mass murder. [14]

Picturing God in the dark room of faith sometimes means that our projections of Her can be difficult to see. We often project our own images of God onto the divine, in effect creating a God who reflects our priorities. This is a true today as it was back in the times of the Old Testament. And that is ok, because God can still work through our projections and mis-projections. Love, reconciliation and justice can emerge even through the blurred pictures we create.

---

[14] Philip Zimbardo, *The Lucifer Effect: How Good People Turn Evil* (London: Rider, 2007), 230.

In the context of a primitive warrior tribe, it was common to worship a warrior God. A God who was on your side and could win you battles would be worthy of devotion and worship.

The writers and editors of the sections of the Old Testament we are going to look at were conditioned by the socio-political context in which they were writing. Many of the texts we will look at were edited and redacted during the Babylonian exile, and there was therefore a desire to write history with 'God on our side'. A God who would give you success in battle when you were obedient, but punish you with defeat and exile when not.

This pattern shows an ancient process whereby primitive tribal societies developed an ethics of right and wrong, of consequence and responsibility. It is no surprise that their projections of God were often of a warrior God. This image was to evolve and be progressively subjected to profound questioning, not just in later books of the Bible, but also at the time that they were written. The command to love the neighbour and look after the stranger feature from the earliest writings of the Torah, and we should bear this in mind as we engage with more problematic texts. Augustine said that when there was an argument over how to interpret a particular passage the principle of charity should inform the final interpretation:

Scripture enjoins nothing but love, and censures nothing but lust, and moulds men's minds accordingly [...] By love I mean the impulse of one's mind to enjoy God on his own account and to enjoy one's neighbour on account of God; and by lust I mean the impulse of one's mind to enjoy oneself and one's neighbour and any corporeal thing not on account of God.[15]

---

[15] St Augustine, *Book III: On Christian Doctrine*, translated by R.P.H. Green. (Oxford University Press), 85-86. (www.pericaritatem.com/2008/02/02/St-

If you are anything like me, then you will have struggled with the image of God portrayed in certain parts of the Old Testament. Even the biblical heroes like Abraham, Moses, Joshua and King David (just to pick a few) engage in behaviour that would be deemed to be abhorrent by any decent human being. In *The God Delusion*, Dawkins rightfully expresses humane revulsion at the so called 'terror passages' of the Old Testament, and the implications they have for God if we are to take them at face value:

The God of the Old Testament is arguably the most unpleasant character in all fiction: jealous and proud of it; a petty, unjust, unforgiving control-freak; a vindictive, bloodthirsty ethnic cleanser; a misogynistic, homophobic, racist, infanticidal, genocidal, filicidal, pestilential, magalomaniacal, sadomasochistic, capriciously malevolent bully.[16]

There is not the space here to give a detailed and contextualised picture of every 'challenging' passage in the Old Testament. Such an enterprise would inevitably run into many volumes. Instead, I am just going to confine my examples to a few well-known characters and narratives within the Old Testament. Although these characters are well known, most Christian preachers and writers have tended to focus on the positive traits of their characters and stories (for obvious reasons), often air-brushing out the difficult and uncomfortable parts. For example, king David is portrayed in children's books as the small boy confronting the evil giant Goliath, but I have never heard a sermon preached, or seen a representation of David

---

Augustine-the-principle-of charity. Ex scripture explicanada est.) accessed 24.09.2015.
[16] Richard Dawkins, *The God Delusion* (London: Black Swan, 2006), 51.

commanding his army to attack a city, deliberately accessing the weakest entry point by massacring the lame and disabled, as is recounted in 2 Samuel 5:6-10, which we will consider later in this chapter. Nor have I ever heard a preacher base his or her sermon on 2 Samuel 4:12, where David commands his men to kill Rachan and Baanah (also murderers, it must be said) and to cut off their limbs and hang their bodies in a public place beside lake Hebron (more on this later). As I write, ISIS (the so-called Islamic State) are performing similar acts of brutality in Northern Iraq against the Yazidi and Christian minorities, whilst also attacking Shia mosques and killing Muslims who do not subscribe to their particular interpretation of the Qur'an.

Or take the example of Moses, who is rightly portrayed as the great freedom fighter liberating the children of Israel from 400 years of slavery in Egypt, but I have yet to hear a sermon where the latter section of Exodus 32 is extolled. In that passage he commands all 'who are on the Lord's side', to go through camp killing 'his brother and his companion and his neighbour' (Exodus 32:26-27). And the Levitical priesthood are the first to volunteer to carry out this apparently divinely sanctioned massacre.

With characters such as Abraham, something even more disturbing is done. It is not that the difficult parts of his character are left out, instead they justified and extolled as virtuous because they exemplify obedience and unquestioning 'faith'. I am of course referring to the story of the sacrifice of Isaac. Or think of the story of Noah, where God is depicted as sending the floods to wipe out his creation?

If you are anything like me, you will have read these stories and felt that the God you worship is very different from the kind of deity depicted in these primitive narratives. If you have children or if you are a Sunday school teacher, maybe you have read through children's Bible stories, and felt horrified. You may have felt compelled to constantly apologise about what you have read.

And then there are of course literally dozens of passages where the God of the Old Testament is depicted in ways that seem to fit with Dawkin's description, cited earlier in this chapter.

When I was growing up as a child, I was taught a song, the lyrics of which went like this 'the grand old book (meaning the Bible), the grand old book, you'll find a word of comfort, wherever you may look, in sorrow and in pain, its promise is the same so keep on believing in the grand old book'. With the tune still ringing in my ears, here is a list (by no means exhaustive) of terror passages in the Bible; a testimony to finding profound 'discomfort' in 'the grand old book'. Here are some examples:

God sending the plagues in Exodus chapters 7-11, God killing the first-born in Exodus 12:29, the destruction of the Amalikites at the hand of Joshua in Exodus 17:13, the permission of slave owners to beat their slaves in Exodus 21:20-21, the promise in Leviticus 26:7-8 that if they are obedient their enemies will die by the sword, the threat that The Lord would send wild beasts amongst them to rob them of their children in Leviticus 26:22 (and later in this same chapter it states that God will punish them by having them eat the flesh of their sons and daughters, see verse 29). In Numbers 15:32-36 Moses (following God's instructions) commands that a man who had broken the Sabbath laws and collected sticks for firewood be stoned to death. The whole congregation joined in the public stoning.

In the following chapter (16:27-33) men, children and their households are swallowed up by the earth at the command of God (and later in this same passage he sends a plague that kills just short of 15,000 people). In Numbers 25:4 Moses orders for 'the chiefs of the people' to be impaled in the sun, and a few verses later Aaron takes a spear and kills an Israelite and his Midianite companion for taking a wife from another people-group.

In Numbers 31:17-18 (with chilling parallels to similar circumstances surrounding his own birth) Moses orders that all the male Midianite children be killed (in addition to every woman who had slept with a man). Later in this chapter 32,000 virgins are kidnapped by the Israelites (not that different from the recent abduction of young girls by the Islamist militants Boko Haram in Northern Nigeria, as I write this book in 2014). In verse 18 of this chapter it states that the young girls who have been spared death are to be kept for the soldiers. Numbers 31:17-18 reads:

Now therefore, kill every male among the little ones, and kill every woman who has known a man by sleeping with him. But all the young girls who have not known a man by sleeping with him, keep alive for yourselves.

Genocide and destruction is commanded in Deuteronomy 7:2, followed some chapters later by the chilling command in Deuteronomy 20:16 which reads 'But as for the towns of these people that The Lord your God is giving to you as an inheritance, you must not let anything that breathes remain alive'. In Deuteronomy 28:53 it mentions the eating of the flesh of children whom 'the Lord your God has given you': 'In desperate straits to which the enemy siege reduces you, you will eat the fruit of your womb, the flesh of your own sons and daughters whom The Lord your God has given to you'. Some may argue that God is simply warning them of what will happen, rather than approving it, but if that is the case, a little more clarification would have been helpful...

In Joshua 6:21 Joshua destroys the city of Jericho, killing men, women and children. Later in Joshua 7:19-26 a whole family (including children) are stoned to death because their father had broken the law, and in Joshua 8:22-25 Joshua carries out a genocide of 12,000 people (including women and children). In Joshua 10 the genocidal ethnic cleansing (sanctioned and ordained by God) wipes out the Gibeonites (verses 10-27), the Makkedah people in verse 28, the Libnahites in verse 30, the Lachish in verses 32-33, the Eglonites in verses 34-35, the Hebronites in verses 36-37, the Debirites in verses 38-39, culminating in Joshua 10:40 with states: 'So Joshua defeated the whole land, the hill country and the Negev and the lowland and the slopes, and all their kings; he left no one remaining, but utterly destroyed all that breathed, as The Lord God of Israel commanded'.

The killing and ethnic cleansing continues. In Joshua 11:21-23 the Anakim people are wiped out at the hand of Joshua. In Judges 1:4 Judah kills 10,000 Canaanites, and verse 6 condones bodily mutilation with chilling resonances to Sharia law. A few chapters later in Judges 3:29 the Israelites kill 10,000 Moabites, and in chapter 7:19-25 the Midianites are killed, and their heads brought back as trophies to Gideon. Then there is Samson, arguably the first suicide terrorist who takes his own life together with those of 3000 others. Later on we read the horrific story of the woman Tamar recounted in Judges 19, who is raped through the night and her body mutilated and sent throughout the tribes of Israel. I have yet to hear a worship song based on Tamar, Graham Kendrick wouldn't go there (if you are reading this Graham, which I very much doubt, I am laying down the musical gauntlet...).

Judges 19 recounts a horrific story of rape, murder and mutilation. In Judges 20 around 25,000 men are put to death (and their villages burnt to the ground) at the hand of the Israelites, in fairness as a 'tit for tat' retaliation in the face of thousands of Israeli deaths. In Judges 21:10-12 the Israelites are commanded to slaughter men, women and children residing in Jabesh-Gilded, and are then instructed to return with 400 virgins which they can keep for their own use. In 1 Samuel 15:3, Saul is commanded to slay the Amalekites, together with women, children and all the animals, and later in verse 33 of that same chapter Samuel mutilates Agag 'before the lord'. In 1 Samuel 18:7 the unrelenting carnage at the hands of Saul and David inspires a group of women to sing 'Saul has slain his thousands, and David his ten thousands', and in 1 Samuel 27:8-11 it clearly states that David had no mercy, but also killed women and children. There are at least another dozen similar incidents in 1 Samuel alone, and I will not list them all, as I think by now you are getting the picture. In 2 Samuel 8:5 David kills 22,000 Arameans, and in verse 13 he kills 18,000 Edomites, and those who are not killed are taken as slaves. In 2 Samuel 10:18 over 47,000 Syrians are slaughtered. 2 Samuel 13:1-15 tells the horrific story of another Tamar, who is raped by her very own brother and then, as if this isn't horrific enough, is punished further by him. In 2 Samuel 18:6-7, 20,000 men are slaughtered. 70,000 men are killed by a plague sent by God, in 2 Samuel 24:15, and in 1 Kings 20:29-30 over 100,000 Atameans are killed by the Israelites. In 2 Kings 2:23-24 forty two children are mauled to death (apparently commanded by God) because the essentially call Elisha 'baldy head' (I once heard one of my conservative Theology lecturers justify this from the point of view that they were not children, but probably young men of adolescent age). I know that adolescent boys can be particularly irksome, but even so, this seems to be a bit of an over-reaction.

In 2 Kings 6:29, a child is cooked and eaten, although there is no mention of God here, so maybe it is just a record of something that happened but which was not sanctioned by God.

In 2 Kings 19:35 an Angel of The Lord kills 185,000 men. In Isaiah 13:15-16 it talks about women being 'ravished' and 'infants dashed to pieces' and in chapter 14:21-22 the slaughter of children is commanded as punishment. In Isaiah 49:26 there is a suggestion that God commands cannibalism, and in Ezekiel 6:12-13 God slays people who worship idols and sends his wrath. Further on in Ezekiel 9:6 we read the chilling words 'cut down old men, young men and young women, little children and women, but touch no one who has the mark. And begin at my sanctuary'. In Ezekiel 20:26 the Israelites sacrifice their own children, and in Hosea 13:16 it reads 'Samaria shall bear her guilt, because she has rebelled against her God; they shall fall by the sword; their little ones shall be dashed in pieces, and their pregnant women ripped open'.

I still have the tune ringing in my head, 'the grand old book, the grand old book, you'll find a word of comfort wherever you may look ...'

I could go on, but I think you get the point....One of the things that strikes me about being reminded of terror passages such as these is that even Christians who believe in the inerrancy of the Bible and that every word is 'God-breathed' and to be taken at face value, do not actually follow through with their convictions. This group of Christians often criticise the more liberal wing of the church (and I don't like the conservative/liberal dualism as it is far too simplistic) for being selective with the Bible, and for only believing the bits they want to, when in fact this is precisely what they do. Although they claim every verse to be the 'word of God', in reality they don't practise this, and they approach the Bible with a highly selective agenda, seldom preaching on the terror passages. In fact, one of my arguments will be that a non-literalist and contextualised approach to the Bible actually gives the text more respect, and enables the enquirer to engage with every verse of scripture and to learn ethical and moral lessons from it, not least from the so-called terror passages.

How does all of this fit with a God who commands in Exodus 20:13 'Thou shall not murder' or 'kill' as it says in the Bible footnote.

Some Christians justify killing by arguing that this verse prohibits murder. My question to them is: 'how many people must be murdered before it becomes killing'? Or is it about motive, and whether or not there is any 'justification' for killing? What is the cut-off point? If I kill one person, that presumably counts as murder, what about if I kill two, three, or more? Or is it about intent? Or whether I am following orders? If a democratic government sanctions killing 'x' in the context of war, is that killing but not murder? To the person being killed it probably feels much the same... If I kill with 'the law' behind me is it killing? If I do it through my own initiative it is murder?

What do we do with narratives such as these? What are our ethical obligations with these texts? Can violence ever be sacralised? Is there an angry and vengeful God hiding behind Christ? Or is this an illusion we have painted? Is God truly revealed in these passages? Or are these passages human pictures of God? Constructs of God as we have created him in our own violent image? Are these stories recorded to remind us about the perils of using religion to justify ethnic cleansing, massacre of innocents and genocide?

Theologian Hans de Wit who has specialised on Latin American hermeneutical processes, has looked at the idea of biblical terror passages as trauma processing. Much of his research focuses on intercultural readings of the Bible, which can bring beneficial effects to the reading communities who engage with them:

> Holy Scripture—not only the Qur'an—is at this time often associated with terror and destruction. It is often suggested in this context that the relation between sacred texts and one's actions is one to one. On the basis of experiences that we have already had, about which I will speak shortly, there is reason to test the hypothesis that the intercultural reading of narratives from sacred texts—in our case, the Bible—can have a beneficial effect and can help readers to have more understanding for one another, to reconciliation and more justice.[17]

The fact that these passages were recorded and included in the canonical scriptures in the first place is of interest in itself. As I write this, so-called Islamic State are posting online videos of beheadings of Christians, Yazidis and Muslims they don't agree with, and justifying their actions buy believing that they are mandated from God. There is a long tradition of justifying and committing violence in the name of God. These are some of the questions and issues I would like to address in the course of this brief chapter, by taking another look at some of the better known stories in the Bible, which at face value portray God in terms not that dissimilar to what Dawkins articulated in *The God Delusion*.

---

[17] Hans de Wit, '"My God", she said, "Ships make me so crazy": Reflections on Empirical Hermeneutics, Interculturality, and Holy Scripture'. Www.Bible4all.org/be stander/documented/ashx?document-if=33 (accessed 24/9/2915)

Noah and the flood

The story of the flood recorded in Genesis chapters 6-8 is not an original or new story, but borrows heavily on pre-existing Babylonian mythology. Most religions have some sort of flood narrative, which makes sense in a pre-scientific age where the natural elements are believed to be directed by the gods. The account in Genesis is no different in this regard, as it depicts God as sending the flood as punishment for the wickedness of the people he had created. The story is so well known that it is hardly necessary to be repeated here.

What I will argue in this section is that what makes the Genesis flood narrative interesting, is not that in itself it is original (it did not drop from the sky, if you can excuse the pun), but it is interesting for how it not only bears significant similarities to ancient Babylonian mythology, but how it differentiates from them. It is in the differentiation where the inspiration lies, not in the idea that it was written ex-nihilo, as it were.

The Genesis account draws heavily on the Gilgamesh epic, which is a narrative poem from Mesopotamia, which predates Genesis by at least several hundred years in terms of its composition. The Gilgamesh account is recorded on clay tablet XI, and written in Akkadian cuneiform. But it is widely believed that the Gilgamesh epic is not the original source for the flood narrative, but it draws heavily on Atra-Hasis Akkadian epic, that dates from around 18th BCE. Tablet III of the Atra-Hasis is what is of interest to us here, as it narrates the story of the god Enki who forewarns Atrahasis that the god Enlil is going to send a flood to destroy mankind, and that he should dismantle his house and build a boat to escape. Similar to the Genesis account, Atrahasis takes his family and animals onto the boat. The flood lasts for seven days, after which Atrahasis tries to appease the gods by offering sacrifices, but to no avail, because unlike Yaweh in the Genesis account, the gods continue to devise ways of destroying mankind.

The Gilgamesh epic, inspired by the Atra-Hasis myth, tells the story of the Babylonian god Enlil who has become angry with humankind because they are making too much noise, so he decides to send a flood to destroy not only them but the whole world (animals and plants included). He tries to enlist the help of other gods in his destructive enterprise, but one of the gods (named Ea) does not comply. Instead he warns Up-Napishtim (a human being), and in a dream tells him to build an ark to save a selection of humans and animals. Here is an extract:

In those days the world teemed, the people multiplied, the world bellowed like a wild bull, and the great god was aroused by the clamor. Enlil heard the clamor and he said to the gods in council, 'The uproar of mankind is intolerable and sleep is no longer possible by reason of the babel {everyone talking at once}.' So the gods agreed to exterminate mankind.

Enlil did this, but Ea warned me in a dream. He whispered their words to my house of reeds, "Reed-house, reed-house! Wall, O wall, hearken reed-house, wall reflect; O man of Shurrupak, son of Ubara-Tutu; tear down your house and build a boat, abandon possessions and look for life, despise worldly goods and save your soul alive. Tear down your house, I say, and build a boat. These are the measurements of the barque {boat} as you shall build her: let her beam equal her length, let her deck be roofed like the vault that covers the abyss; then take up into the boat the seed of all living creature.[18]

Similar to the Genesis account, in the Gilgamesh birds are sent out to check for dry land (a raven, a swallow and a dove, similar to Genesis 8: 6-8 when Noah first sends out a

---

[18]*The Gilgamesh Epic,* translated by N.K.Sanders (Hammondsworth: Penguin, 1972), 108-109.

raven, followed by a dove). In both the Gilgamesh and Genesis the Ark rests on top of a mountain.

But both the Atrahasis and the Gilgamesh accounts are inspired directly by an even earlier flood narrative, and bear striking similarities, simply known as the 'Sumerian Creation Myth', and sometimes referred to as the 'Eridu Genesis'. The flood lasts for seven days and seven nights, halting only when the sun god 'Utu' arrives. The story ends with Zid-ud-sura (the equivalent of Noah) offering sacrifices of sheep and oxen, which is likely to be the foundational source inspiration for Genesis 8:20 where Noah also offers animal sacrifices to God ('Then Noah built an altar to The Lord and took of every clean animal and of every clean bird and offered burnt offerings on the altar' Genesis 8:20).

Even after a very brief conspectus of these various flood myths, the similarities with the Genesis account are there for all to see. Much has been written on this subject, and for those interested in pursuing it further there are a wealth of sources providing fascinating detail and analysis. But what interests me about these ancient myths, is not only their similarities, but crucially the issue of differentiation. What is striking about the Genesis account of the flood is its differentiation from its Sumerian and Babylonian textual forebears. The main difference is that the Genesis account presents a monotheistic view of the divine. As any anthropologist or historian of ancient religions would tell you, monotheism is a relatively late arrival on the religious stage. The earliest religions were polytheistic. Monotheism emerges later. What the Genesis account shows are the dilemmas and struggles of a faith-based society that has transitioned and evolved away from polytheism to monotheism.[19] In ancient societies that existed long before the emergence of modern science, it was believed that natural elements and weather patterns were sent by the Gods. So when the sun shone and the crops grew, the gods were happy with you, whereas when natural disasters happened (be it severe droughts, hurricanes or floods) then the gods were angry with you, and needed to be appeased through sacrificial rites (as all the flood narratives show). When you transition to monotheism, you have a real conundrum to sort out, because you no longer have the sun-god and the rain-god commanding the elements, but both are rolled into one. Yahweh sends both blessing and curse, judgement and mercy. The Noah narrative shows this essential characteristic of monotheistic Judaism.

The other main point of differentiation is that the Genesis account ends with reconciliation and the (in the Atrahasis account) the gods do not reconcile with human beings, but devise new forms of punishment.

There is real moment of epiphanic revelation in the much ignored verse of Genesis 9:6 which is one of the foundational truths for Judaism and later for Judeo-Christianity which reads: 'Whoever sheds the blood of a human, by a human shall that person's blood be shed, for in his own image, God has made humankind'.

Had this mandate been followed, there would have been no ethnic cleansing by Joshua, no massacre in the camp at the hands of Moses, not attacking of the city by targeting the weak and the lame by King David... and no wars. Surely Jesus the Rabbi was being true to his roots

---

[19] I am grateful to my friend Reverend Marjory McPherson for this insight, during a conversation overlooking a Scottish loch at the home of some mutual friends.

when he responded in non-violence to those who crucified him? When he told Peter to put away the sword, when he responded to his killers with healing (represented in the healing of the soldier's ear) rather than with vengeance?

In the light of this inspired text, this moment of transcendent epiphany, which carries more divine weight than any of the other terror texts referenced above, is what eventually won out against the myriad misrepresentations of God that were to follow. Surely this text must be understood (given its place so early on in the biblical canon) as foundational, calling us to see the other as made in the image of God, and therefore imbued with dignity and worth?

It is little wonder then, that when subsequent generations of men in the history of Israel (Moses, Joshua, Caleb, Samuel, Saul, David, Jonathan and numerous others) committed heinous acts of murder, ethnic cleansing and genocide, the only way they could justify it (and convince others to join in with the killing spree), was by invoking God. Justifying violence through religion, which throughout history has been (and continues to be) its major downfall.

Had God changed his mind, from the clear prohibition given to Noah in Genesis 9:6?

The Sacrifice of Isaac
I was brought up with this story from an early age. At the age of eleven I even acted out the part of Abraham in a school play, and I remember raising the knife above the head of one of my classmates who was lying stretched out on the altar, only to then hear the voice of God pointing me to a lamb caught in a thicket. Although Abraham relents from sacrificing his son at the last moment, I

49

always found it disturbing that someone who was prepared to do this was then immortalised as a hero in the monotheistic religions. Are the newspapers not full of stories of atrocities carried out by those who claim to have heard God's voice? Even as a child, I struggled with the idea of making someone a hero because of his unquestioning obedience to God, especially if it meant killing his son.

I have heard various 'explanations' and 'justifications' of this story. Before I detail the most common of these, is there not something absurd and even deranged about having to 'explain' or 'justify' God? Surely this is not really compatible with loving someone? It would be bizarre in the extreme for someone having to explain or justify Mother Teresa, Martin Luther King, or Ghandi. So why do it with God?

One of the 'justifications' for Abraham's willingness to kill his son uses belief in the resurrection as justification. Basically, because Abraham was a man of faith, and believed in the resurrection (leaving aside the issue that most in the Old Testament would have had no concept of the after-life) he would have been justified in killing his son as God could have raised him back to life.

Even taking this at face value, what kind of a God would demand this? What degree of sycophantic power-play would need to be involved? What about the suffering and trauma of Isaac being subjected to the knife at the hands of his father? What about the grief of Abraham, and the roller-coaster emotions (assuming for a moment that Isaac would have then been resurrected)?

Another explanation is provided by philosopher Soren Kierkegaard. Whilst I have a lot of time for Kierkegaard's highly creative philosophical writings, his conclusion regarding the Sacrifice of Isaac which he expounds in *Fear and Trembling* is, in my opinion, not only deeply flawed, but morally and ethically dangerous. There is not the time or space to go into this in much detail here, but essentially, what Kierkegaard does is to differentiate and separate the sphere of ethics from that of religion. According to Kierkegaard Abraham engages in a 'teleological suspension of the ethical', that is, that he decides to 'obey God' because this is right on religious grounds, but in order to do so it necessitates suspending all ethical judgement. Kierkegaard writes 'Abraham believed and did not doubt; he believed the preposterous'. Abraham acts by virtue of the absurd, for the absurd is precisely that he as the single individual is higher than the universal [...] By his act he transcended the whole of the ethical and had a higher telos outside, in relation to which he suspended it.'[20]

No matter how you attempt to dress this up with clever and nuanced philosophy, the argument is deeply flawed on several levels. First of all, you can never divide so-called religious motives/acts from ethical motive/ acts; as every choice we make as human beings has ethical implications (for good or bad) on both ourselves and those around us. Secondly, to divest religious acts from the sphere of ethics (even though Kierkegaard would say that this is only done because of an absolute faith in God that he/she cannot do anything evil) is highly dangerous. What is happening across the globe in terms of Islamist extremism follows a similar logic, where beheadings, suicide bombings deliberately targeting the innocent, the burning alive of Christians in churches, Shiite Muslims in mosques, and the abduction and abuse of young girls, is only possible because all ethical frameworks have been divorced from real religious conviction (which would prohibit such

---

[20] Soren Kierkegaard, *Fear and Trembling,* edited by C. Stephens Evans & Sylvia Walsh. Translated by Sylvia Walsh (Cambridge: Cambridge U.P., 2006), 17, 46, 49, 52.

violence), and justified by a misuse of religious fanatical belief system coupled with a rejection of any humane ethical considerations. Kierkegaard's explanation will simply not do.

I remember once listening to Leonard Cohen's song 'The story of Isaac', and thinking that Cohen's understanding of the event made more sense. Rather than blaming God, or trying to justify God, it places responsibility back on us as human beings. It calls for us to question our motives. It demands that we weigh up the ethical implications of what it means to 'hear God's voice'. In calls us to question what we do when we do it in 'the name of God'. How can we be sure? Many of you will know the song, but here are the lyrics:

The story of Isaac (Leonard Cohen)

The door it opened slowly,
My father he came in,
I was nine years old.
And he stood so tall above me,
His blue eyes they were shining
And his voice was very cold.
He said, 'I've had a vision
And you know I'm strong and holy,
I must do what I've been told'.
So he started up the mountain,
I was running, he was walking,
And his axe was made of gold.

Well, the trees they got much smaller,
The lake a lady's mirror,
We stopped to drink some wine.
Then he threw the bottle over.
Broke a minute later
And he put his hand on mine.

Warrior God

Thought I saw an eagle
But it might have been a vulture,
I never could decide.
Then my father built an altar,
He looked once behind his shoulder,
He knew I would not hide.

You who build these altars now
To sacrifice these children,
You must not do it anymore.
A scheme is not a vision
And you never have been tempted
By a demon or a god.
You who stand above them now,
Your hatchets blunt and bloody,
You were not there before,
When I lay upon a mountain
And my father's hand was trembling
With the beauty of the world.

And if you call me brother now,
Forgive me if I inquire,
'Just according to whose plan?'
When it all comes down to dust
I will kill you if I must,
I will help you if I can.
When it all comes down to dust
I will help you if I must,
I will kill you if I can.
And mercy on our uniform,
Man of peace or man of war,
The peacock spreads his fan.

Cohen's song in my mind goes to the very heart of the matter because it reminds us that to be human is to question, to doubt. If we were not capable of this, we would be mere automatons, acting out a predetermined script, with no ability for ethical choice. The song depicts how doubt is part of everyday life, as Isaac spots a bird of prey on his ascent up the mountain: 'Thought I saw an eagle, but it might have been a vulture, I never could decide.' Cohen reminds us that as human beings, perceiving what is to be truth is problematic. Our minds can play tricks on us, things are seldom clear-cut. Isaac is not sure about whether he has seen an eagle or a vulture. How can his father Abraham be sure that he is hearing God correctly? The implication in Cohen's song is how can you be sure that the voice you are hearing inside your head to sacrifice your son is God's voice? How do you differentiate God's voice from that of your own psyche? In Cohen's reading of the story God enters the scene to make clear to Abraham that he does not demand child sacrifice.

History is a stark reminder of the many evils done and justified in the name of God, and this story in Genesis is a timely reminder of the inherent dangers of justifying the unjustifiable by claiming to have heard 'the voice of God'.

But there is a very different reading to this story. One, which I believe, radically transforms the image of Yahweh from the deity who demands blood sacrifice to one who wants its end. Abraham was a nomad and a tent-dweller. He was on the move and coming into contact with many ancient religious traditions. Anthropology shows us that some ancient religions practised ritual child sacrifice. In Abraham's day sacrificing your son to the gods would not have been altogether uncommon. And yet in the Hebraic tradition the sacrifice of children to gods is strictly forbidden and outlawed. In Leviticus it clearly denounces offering children to the god of Molech, the fire God. In Leviticus 18:21 it categorical states: 'You shall not give any of your offspring to sacrifice them to Molech, and so profane the name of your God: I am The Lord'. Molech was a brass figure, half calf half human, known as the fire god and was worshipped in Canaanite and Syrian religions. Priests would light a fire and place babies into Molech's hand as a sacrifice. The Leviticus text denounces this practice in a direct and unambiguous way. Ancient Jewish religion was to be based on the loving of one's neighbour, and the prohibition of killing. In this context, Abraham's willingness to sacrifice his son has much more in keeping with Canaanite religious practices than it does with ancient Judaism. And herein lies the key to this story.

Yahweh differentiates himself from the Canaanite gods. This is a story about differentiation. Abraham believes he has heard God asking him to sacrifice his son, influenced by Canaanite religion. Yahweh steps in to bring this barbaric practice to an end, and so in a very public way, thus differentiating himself from the other gods. Yahweh will be the God who does not demand blood sacrifice, but progressively brings about its end. The story of Abraham and Isaac is about a moving away not only from infanticide but also from the demands for blood sacrifice. We will discuss the latter more fully in the next chapter of this book.

Moses and the massacre in the camp

In this section I want to examine the problematic ending of Exodus 32. This passage of scripture opens up questions about human choices and responsibility. As a framework for considering the passage I would like to reference the important work of Phillip Zimbardo. The relevance of referencing Zimbardo's work before engaging with Exodus 32, will, I hope, become clear.

In Philip Zimbardo's book *The Lucifer Effect: How Good People Turn Evil,* quoted at the beginning of this chapter, he comments on the ground-breaking research of psychologist and Yale professor Stanley Milgram. The research experiment he carried out has become so well known that it is now simply referred to as 'The Milgram Experiment'. I will now go on to paraphrase Zimbardo's excellent summary, but those of you interested in looking more deeply into this should read his much more detailed account quoted above.[21]

Milgram's experiment started off in the early 1960s. It was a time when the world was still trying to come to terms with the recent memory of the Holocaust, which rightly provoked profound questioning across the field of science and the humanities about the capacity for human evil. It is no coincidence that at the time of Milgram's experiment, the trail of the Nazi War criminal Adolf Eichmann was a high profile case being reported in the media across the globe. He had been tracked to his hiding place in Argentina by Mossad, Israel's secret police, and put on trial in Jerusalem. This is the trial that was to be so influential for Hannah Arendt, who I would urge you to read on the question of evil, if you haven't already come across her work.

In theological disciplines, the question of how to do theology after Auschwitz was being asked, as the idea of an omnipotent and yet benevolent God was being called in to question, eloquently expressed in Yehuda Amichai's poem 'After Auschwitz':

NOVEMBER 1999

AFTER AUSCHWITZ

by Yehuda Amichai
translated by Chana Bloch and Chana Kronfeld

---

[21] Phillip Zimbardo, *The Lucifer Effect: How Good People Turn Evil* (London: Rider, 2009).

After Auschwitz, no theology:
From the chimneys of the Vatican, white smoke rises –
a sign the cardinals have chosen themselves a Pope.
From the crematoria of Auschwitz, black smoke rises –
a sign the conclave of Gods hasn't yet chosen
the Chosen People.
After Auschwitz, no theology:
the inmates of extermination bear on their forearms
the telephone numbers of God,
numbers that do not answer
and now are disconnected, one by one.

After Auschwitz, a new theology:
the Jews who died in the Shoah
have now come to be like their God,
who has no likeness of a body and has no body.
They have no likeness of a body and they have no body.[22]

Milgram's experiment emerged as a direct response to the Holocaust, in the attempt to come to a greater understanding of how human beings can be capable of carrying of carrying out orders that lead to unspeakable suffering when instructed to do so by figures in positions of authority. Milligram's experiment invited volunteers to participate in what they believed to be research into improving people's memory and learning capacities. The volunteers were paid to take part, and told that they were enabling a vital research exercise of real importance and significance. The volunteers were taken into a scientific lab, and were explained how the experiment would work: basically each volunteer would draw straws to determine who would play the role of the 'teacher' and who would be the 'learner'. The learner was given a series of word

---

[22] Yehuda Amichai, 'Auschwitz'. www.the
atlantic.com/past/docs/unbound/petty/anthology/Amichai/auschwitz.htm
(accessed 24.9.2015)

association exercises, which involved memory and the ability to pair words correctly through association. Depending on whether the learner responded correctly or not, they would be given verbal encouragement by the teacher or administered an electric shock as punishment for getting the answer wrong. The experiment was of course rigged in such a way that the volunteer always ended up playing the role of teacher. The learner (who was always an actor) was connected up to an electrode in the next room, but the 'teacher' and the researcher in the white coat directing the experiment could communicate with the learner through an intercom system. The shock generator (which of course did not administer real shocks) had a series of different switches which supposedly could administer a whole range of shocks from mild to life-threatening intense ones. Once the experiment begins, the 'learner' (and actor hooked up to the shock machine) gives a few correct answers, but then deliberately continues to make mistakes. The 'teacher', instructed by the authority figure of the researcher present in the room, is continually instructed to administer increasingly severe electric shocks to the learner, even though the teacher can hear that the learner is in real pain. What is interesting about this experiment, is that in the vast majority of cases, what Miligram observed was that the 'teachers' followed the instructions to administer increasing levels of electric shocks, even when the suffering of the learner was clear to them. When a teacher protested and questioned whether they should continue because they felt uncomfortable with the suffering of the learner, the researcher in the white coat reminded them of the contract, and also of the importance of the research that would bring long term benefits for learning and research. Even when the teacher could no longer hear the protestations of the learner (and assumed him to be unconscious), two out of every three 'teachers' would administer the deadly shock, as long as it was made clear to them that they were not personally responsible in the event of the learner dying. Being reassured by the researcher that they would take responsibility in such an event, most went on to administer the maximum shock.

One of the things that Milgram's experiment showed, was how normal human beings (not psychopaths or mentally deranged individuals) were capable of inflicting huge suffering by willingly participating in a system, as long as they were not ultimately responsible. As long as they were following instructions by a figure of authority (in this case the scientist in the white coat) who was in charge, most would comply with the instructions.

Miligram's experiment had huge implications for our understanding of how much of the German population were to become active participants in the machinery of the Third Reich, through a system of obeying orders passed down from figures in positions of power and authority. The modern systems of communication through telephone and radio, and the effective bureaucratic structures, provided a system of communication and control whereby individuals became complicit agents. Decades earlier, the Jewish-Czech author Franz Kafka, had written a novel which highlighted the dangers of mass bureaucratic systems where individuals 'were just doing their jobs'. In his novel *The Trial*, the protagonist Joseph K. is arrested in his bed one morning, but he does not know why, and much of the novel is about Joseph K. trying the prove his innocence, but continually comes up against a system populated by individuals who are just carrying out orders and doing their job. His life is turned into a nightmare because nobody questions the orders they are carrying out, and without failure, place the responsibility for their actions the elsewhere. *The Trial* provides a chilling prophecy of what was to happen in 1930s and 40s Germany, and of how normal people working within the bureaucratic modern-state machinery were to become complicit participators, acquiescing to the regulations and codes of conduct of the apparatus of State control.

What Zimbardo concluded from Miligram's research was that:

The data clearly revealed the extreme pliability of human nature: almost everyone could be totally obedient or almost everyone could resist authority pressures. It all depended on the situational variables they experienced. Miligram was able to demonstrate that compliance rates would soar over 90 percent of people continuing the 450-volt maximum or be reduced to less than 10 percent—by introducing just one crucial variable into the compliance recipe.[23]

Miligram's research is highly relevant when we come to reading parts of the Bible where God apparently orders/sanctions violence. The passage of Exodus 32 which we will now consider, details how Moses commands the violence in the camp by directly appealing to divine authority, and according to the text God later, sends a plague to finish off any survivors from the massacre, so Moses' actions are depicted as being divinely sanctioned.

What better way to avoid taking personal responsibility for heinous murderous acts when you can convince yourself and those around you that you are following divine orders? Let us consider the text in question.

Those of you who went to Sunday school or who had children's Bibles read to you at bed time will be familiar with the story of the Golden Calf recounted in that all too notorious chapter of Exodus 32. But the probability is that the last section of the chapter (verses 25 onwards) would have been airbrushed out of the story. We all remember

[23] Zimbardo, *The Lucifer Effect*, 272.

the basic narrative. Moses is up the mountain and whilst he is away Aaron and the children of Israel melt down their jewellery and make a golden calf which they begin to worship. Moses comes down the mountain and becomes furious with what he sees, so reacts by commanding a mass slaughter in the name of God. The agents of internecine violence are the Levites no less: the priestly tribe. Because (like so many terror passages in the Old Testament) preachers and children's Bible editors normally avoid the bits they find difficult, here is a reminder of verses 25 to the end of the chapter:

When Moses saw that the people were running wild (for Aaron had let them run wild, to the derision of their enemies), then Moses stood in the gate of the camp and said, 'Who is on the Lord's side? Come to me! And all the sons of Levi gathered around him. He said to them, 'Thus says The Lord, the God of Israel, "Put your sword on your side, each of you! Go back and forth from gate to gate throughout the camp, and each of you kill your brother, your friend, and your neighbour"'. The sons of Levi did as Moses commanded, and about three thousand people fell on that day. Moses said, 'Today you have ordained yourselves for the service of The Lord, each one at the cost of a son or brother, and so have brought blessing in yourselves this day'.

On the next day Moses said to the people, 'You have sinned a great sin. But now I will go up to the Lord; perhaps I can make atonement for your sin'. So Moses returned to the Lord and said, 'Alas, this people has sinned a great sin; they have made for themselves gods of gold. But now, if you will only forgive their sin—but if not, blot me out of the book that you have written'. But the Lord said to Moses, 'whoever has sinned against me I will blot out of my book. But now go, lead the people to the place about which I have spoken to you; see my angel shall go in front of you. Nevertheless, when the day comes for punishment, I will punish them for their sin'.

Then the Lord sent a plague on the people, because of what they did with the calf that Aaron made. (Exodus 32:25-35)

History is full of those who have killed in the name of God, who (like Miligram's experiment shows) will carry out atrocities as long as they are not held 'personally responsible', as in their own minds they are innocent, and only carrying out orders from higher powers. Kafka captures this powerfully in his novel *The Trial*, when protagonist Joseph K. questions the two men who arrested him one morning, and they basically justify their actions by not taking personal responsibility because they are following orders. Kafka's novel pointed with chilling prophetic accuracy to what would happen less than 20 years later, when the evil structural machinery of the Third Reich nearly wiped out the Jewish people, and only made possible because everyday normal human beings followed orders, and did not question. Never has C.P. Snow's warning that more evil has been committed in the name of obedience (cited at the beginning of this chapter) been more relevant. There is no time here to go into how an advanced 'Christian' nation which had produced great art, music and philosophy was capable of such evil, except to say that the power to comply and obey rather than question and resist lies at the heart of what went on. Indeed, throughout the New Testament there are two traditions with sit alongside each other: the prophetic apocalyptic tradition (of which Christ is a part) which (in large part because of the Exodus in Egypt and the Babylonian Exile and latterly the Roman Empire) sees power as corrupt and something to resist and subvert; which contrasts with the Pauline tradition which urges citizens to submit and respect those in authority because they are put there by God.

But let us return to Exodus 32, because I want to suggest a different reading, as there is a subtle clue in the text that Moses is acting outside of the moral law, and then attributes responsibility to God by putting words into his mouth.

It is symbolic that before commanding genocide, Moses breaks the tablets of stone. The tablets had just been given to him on Mount Sinai, the sixth commandment of which categorically states 'you shall not murder' (Exodus 20:13). And in Leviticus 19:18' it states: 'You shall not take vengeance or bear a grudge against any of your people, but you shall love your neighbour as yourself: I am the Lord'. Moses acts outside the Law. The breaking of the tablets is a clue in the text that he is now operating not under the guidance of God, but from a place where he is now rejecting the law of God. But this does not stop Moses from claiming that God is on his side, which in his mind (and of many around him) gives him the moral authority to do what he does. And it is harrowing that it is the Levites, the priestly order who obey. Those who had been set aside for worship are the ones who carry out the massacre.

This is not the first instance of Moses acting out of anger and frustration. There is the episode when he strikes the rock twice and no water comes out, because he does it out of anger. It is also significant that he is not allowed to enter the Promised Land, even though he was the main protagonist in liberating the children of Israel from slavery in Egypt.

Exodus 32 shows the danger of how religious power can be terribly abused, and how we must always question our spiritual leaders, who like Moses, can use religion to commit terrible crimes, especially when driven by anger. Narratives such as Exodus 32 can speak truths about ourselves and the societies we live in and construct. It is a warning about what can happen when we operate outside of the law of God, when we smash the tablets of stone which prohibit murder, and then justify our actions by appealing to a higher power so that we are not held responsible.

Joshua: stoning and ethnic cleansing

Joshua 7:18-26 recounts a grim episode in the life of Joshua, and indeed those affected by his actions. The text in question is often referred to as 'The Sin of Achan', although in my view, it should be called 'The disproportionate sins of Joshua and his mob'. Here is the text:

And he brought near his household one by one, and Achan the son of Carmi, son of Zabdi, son of Zerah, of the tribe of Judah, was taken. Then Joshua said to Achan, 'My son, give glory to the LORD God of Israel and make confession to him. Tell me now what you have done; do not hide it from me.' And Achan answered Joshua, 'It is true; I am the one who sinned against the LORD God of Israel. This is what I did: when I saw among the spoil a beautiful mantle from Shinar, and two hundred shekels of silver, and a bar of gold weighing fifty shekels, then I coveted them and took them. They now lie hidden in the ground inside my tent, with the silver underneath'.

So Joshua sent messengers, and they ran to the tent; and there it was, hidden in his tent with the silver underneath. And they took them out of the tent and brought them to Joshua and to all the people of Israel. They took them out of the tent and brought them to Joshua and all the Israelites; and they spread them out before The Lord. Then Joshua and all Israel with him took Achan the son of Zerah, with the silver, the mantle, and the bar of gold, with his sons and daughters, with his oxen, donkeys, and sheep, and his tent and all that he had; and they brought them up to the Valley of Achor. Joshua said, 'Why did you bring trouble on us? The LORD is bringing trouble on you today'. And all Israel stoned him to death; they burned them with fire, cast stones on them, and raised over him a great heap of stones that remains to this day. Then the LORD turned from his burning anger. Therefore that place to this day is called the Valley of Achor.

Here we have another example of murdering in God's name (not that different to what Islamic State are doing in current day Northern Iraq, Syria and the broader Middle

East and Mediterranean). Similar to strands of current Islamist belief, stoning is the brutal means by which Joshua kills not only Achan, but his family, including his sons and daughters, in addition to his livestock. After committing this callous act murder, Joshua and his mob pile stones on top of the burnt corpses, as a kind of memorial, and the redactors and editors of the text chillingly inform the reader that their murderous actions have now made God's anger to turn away.

The conclusion we are led to believe is that God is so angry because of Achan's theft of the gold, silver and clothing; that the only way he can calm himself down is by having Achan's whole family and livelihood stoned and burnt to death. The fact that Joshua's murderous actions break the sixth commandment which forbids murder/killing depending on what translation you use, does not seem to trouble the editors of the book at all. By making out that Joshua's crime is ordained by God neatly bypasses the requirement of following the Ten Commandments.

What this text shows is not a murderous God, but a violent ancient society, carrying out their own form of mob rule, and justifying it as obedience to a higher power. It is highly reminiscent of Miligram's experiment discussed earlier, namely that human beings are more likely to carry out atrocities when they are commanded to do so by someone in a position of authority. This will be something that is confirmed in numerous passages of the Old Testament.

Just because the text says 'the Lord says' or 'the Lord commanded', does not mean that God actually did. It just means that those editing and writing these ancient theological history, believed this. The text illustrates and tells us more about the belief system at the time, rather than about what God is actually like.

But alongside the apparent commandments to kill and plunder in God's name, we have the 'still small voice' (to echo Caputo) alternative voice/ call/ solicitation not to murder, but to love the stranger and to walk in righteousness. It is a tension that will weave itself through the whole of the canon of scripture, and is even present in the gospels, and seem in the famous dialogue between Jesus and Peter just before he is to be crucified. Peter appeals to force, Jesus reveals a better way, that of non-violence., that of blessing those who curse him, and stretching out in forgiveness for the very people who crucify him.

The gospels suggest that even Jesus was tempted by violence. As Andre Trocme reminds us in his book *Jesus and the Non-Violent Revolution*:

Toward the end of his life, the temptation toward violence only increased. Jesus vented his indignation toward the scribes and Pharisees by calling divine vengeance upon them (Matthew 23) [...] The temptation to use violence accompanied Jesus right to his death. A few hours before his arrest he went so far as to reverse his earlier instructions concerning absolute poverty and meekness. 'But now if you have a purse, take it, and also a bag; and if you don't have a sword, sell your cloak and buy one.' When his disciples said, 'See, Lord, here are two swords,' he told them, 'That is enough' (Luke 22:36–38). Beyond these two paltry human weapons, Jesus knew he could count on the help of twelve legions of angels ready to intervene at a moment's notice. It was only after an intense inner struggle, after the genuine moral agony at Gethsemane, that Jesus finally rejected resorting to violence.[24]

---

[24] Andre Trocme, *Jesus and the Non-Violent Revolution* (New York: Plough Publishing House, 2011), 96.

Jesus' triumph came from his sacrificial refusal to meet violence with violence. And he inspired his closest followers and the early church to do the same. All the apostles (except John) were martyred. And the Roman Empire continued to persecute Christians by throwing them into arenas with wild animals, crucifying and torturing them.

It has been said that The Roman Empire was converted to Christianity by the witness of the martyrs.

At the heart of Christianity is the command to love our enemies and not repay evil with evil, but to do justice, and seek reconciliation through sacrificial love. Unfortunately as history shows, the church has not always lived by these foundational truths, but has become too accommodating with power structures, it has lost its prophetic voice in terms of denouncing policies which promote and are complicit in systems of injustice. And because of this it has lost its moral authority.

It is no coincidence that some of the most important social reformers of the past century led movements of non-violent resistance. Ghandi defeated an empire through subversive peaceful non-violent resistance. Martin Luther King changed a nation through his activism, church ministry, preaching and public speaking. Mother Teresa brought dignity and worth to the outcasts and those on the margins, loving through the barriers of religious belief, race or caste.

The church has too often sought for power, and in doing so has lost its authority. The authority of Ghandi, Mother Teresa, Martin Luther King came from a living embodiment of the same self-sacrifical love that characterised Jesus' ministry on earth. They embodied a new way of living. Not seeking after material wealth but after justice, and associating with those on the margins of society and the oppressed.

If the church is going to have any place and relevance in our 21st world, it will be by rediscovering the core message of Christ which calls us to lay down our lives for the sake of others. This means that our worship and adoration of God is lived out in the pursuit of love of others. If we love others, then justice follows out as a direct result. It is impossible to love someone, and at the same time to enslave them. It is impossible to love them, and then kill them. To love is to do justice.

The tragedy is that throughout history the church has sought power through earthly systems and methods, which do not bring true authority because they do not demand us to take up our cross. In fact earthy power operates in the exact opposite direction: through self-aggrandisement, through privilege, self-protection, upward mobility, earthly status, and often a craving for control.

Christ calls us on a downward path of self-emptying.

Resurrection and reconciling love comes not from a place of self-imposed power, but from laying down our lives down in the service of others. It is this self-giving love which we celebrate at the Eucharist which we are called to embody.

The Bible is a history of how ancient societies have understood God. And it is also a selection of texts through which God reveals herself and speaks to her people.

The image of God Joshua had was in the dark room of the camera obscura, where shadows faint signs of image begin to emerge. But when you take what you think is an image that is not yet fully developed, and project it as the final image, you get a different and distorted picture. Later, authors writing the second Isaiah would question the God of Joshua, and paint a very different image associated with the Suffering Servant.

Ethnic cleansing

The chapters of Joshua 1-12 are well known as the conquest narrative of the Promised Land, and the utter destruction of the inhabitants (mandated by God, according to the text). Ethnic cleansing and mass slaughter are carried out in the name of God, and the perpetrators of these crimes are presented as moral examples because of their obedience to God.

Chapters 1-12 are full of divinely sanctioned terror and ethnic cleansing, and although there is not the time now to engage in a detailed analysis of each, let us look at one section of the text, Joshua 11:10-15, to give us a flavour of what was going on:

And Joshua turned back at that time, and took Hazor, and struck its king down with the sword. Before that time Hazor was the head of all those kingdoms. And they put to the sword all who were in it, utterly destroying them; there was none left who breathed, and he burned Hazor with fire. And all the towns of those kings, and all their kings, Joshua took, and struck them with the edge of the sword, utterly destroying them, as Moses the servant of the LORD had commanded. But Israel burned none of the towns that stood on mounds except Hazor, which Joshua did burn. And all the spoil of these towns, and the livestock, the Israelites took for their booty; but all the people they struck down with the edge of the sword, until they had destroyed them, and they did not leave any who breathed. As the LORD had commanded his servant Moses, so Moses commanded Joshua, and so Joshua did; he left nothing undone of all that the LORD had commanded Moses.

It must be remembered that most modern scholarship would be extremely sceptical about attaching any historical credence to these events. But that is not the point. Historical veracity is not what is interesting here. What is of real importance is what these texts tell us about the authors and redactor's view of God and religion. What was it about their context that caused them to depict God as a blood-thirsty warrior? To answer some of these questions we need to remember that the book of Joshua was written long after the purported events it describes, and therefore we need to read the book asking ourselves what does it tell us about the authors view of God. Note also the chain of command: God orders Moses, who obeys and in turn orders Joshua, who obeys and in turn orders his army. There is a clear hierarchical line of command. The atrocities happen because each agent believes himself to not be ultimately responsible, as he is only following orders, and being obedient. Non-questioning obedience was prized higher in that context above all else. Never have C.P. Snow's words been so chillingly relevant.

Most scholars would argue that the book of Joshua was written around the time when Josiah was king (640-609 BC), but it would have been heavily edited and redacted even after that, and not finalised until after 586 BC, which is when Jerusalem was conquered by the Babylonian Empire. Some even argue that it was finished after the children of Israel return from exile in Babylon around 539 BC. Why is this so important?

It is important because the children of Israel had been exiled in a foreign land. They understood this as judgment from God because of disobedience and the breaking of the covenant. The book of Joshua is about the culmination of the Exodus in that it describes the conquering of the Promised Land. The events it purports to recount can be dated to around 13 century BC (although as mentioned earlier, most scholarship does not recognise it as a historical accurate account). Like most ancient religious and mythical literature of the time, God is depicted as the warrior God, who rewards them with victory on the battlefield when they are obedient, but punishes them with destruction and exile when they depart from his ways.

Scholar Karen Armstrong reflects on the brutality of Old Testament figures such as Moses and Joshua, reminding us of the context in which these texts were written and redacted, responding to a context of war and exile:

[...] The eminent scholar Haym Soloveitchik argues that the transition from an oral tradition to written texts can lead to religious stridency by giving the reader an unrealistic certainty about essentially ineffable matters. Deuteronomist religion was certainly strident. The reformers depicted Moses preaching a policy of violent suppression of the native Canaanites [...] They described with approval Joshua massacring the people of Ai as though he were an Assyrian general [...] The Deuteronomists had absorbed the violent ethos of a region that had experienced nearly two hundred years of Assyrian brutality. It was an early indication that scripture reflects the failures as well as the high points of the religious quest.[25]

It is almost so obvious that it doesn't need stating, but the idea of the warrior-god is of course not unique to ancient Israel. The study of ancient literatures and anthropology show how widespread this vision of the gods was. Much of Greek mythology predated the composition of the Old Testament, and there is no question regarding its influence on the biblical texts and on the prevailing culture of the day (Homer's *Odyssey* itself was composed in the late 8th century BC and Homer's *Iliad* is even earlier, some say late 9th century BC). The Homeric hymns,

---

[25] Karen Armstrong, *The Bible: The Biography* (London: Atlantic Books, 2007), 24.

composed around 7 BC, include one to Ares, the god of war. In it he is described as riding on a chariot (reminiscent of Yahweh), and is depicted as a mighty warrior god, driving away the enemy. In this sense it is hardly surprising that the Old Testament is full of depictions of Yahweh as the warrior god. It is in keeping with its time in this regard. In Homer's *Iliad* the warrior god Achilles is depicted as an expert in winning battles, and a god whose wrath is difficult to appease, as seen in the very opening lines of Book I:

Sing, goddess, the wrath of Achilles Peleus' son, the ruinous wrath that brought on the Archaians woes innumerable. And hurled down into Hades many strong souls of heroes, and have their bodies to be prey to dogs and all winged fowls; and so the counsel of Zeus wrought out it accomplishment from the day when first strife parted Astreides king of men and noble Achilles.[26]

In the ancient societies we are discussing, feelings of tribal and ethnic pride would often go hand in hand with military prowess. The book of Joshua is no exception, and is in keeping with the prevailing world mythical literature of its day. But what is interesting in the context of ancient Israel is that the image of a wrathful God is not the only image of God. Instead, there is also a picture of Yahweh who refrains from war and shows mercy. A God who forgives and restores, and shows compassion for the needy and demands justice for the poor (the book of Amos is key here). In Yahweh there is a conflict, and eventually it will be the god of compassion that wins out when we get to the writings of Isaiah (8th century BC, around the same time as Homer). Rabbi Sacks eloquently reminds us of the importance and uniqueness of voices such as that of the Second Isaiah emerging at the time, which represent a radical new way of understanding the divine, a progressive

---

[26] Homer, *The Iliad* (Ware: Wordsworth Classics, 1995), 1.

move away from the prevailing violent images associated with the gods. Sacks argues that you simply do not have voices like those of Isaiah or Jeremiah in the Greek literature of the time, and in this sense the Hebrew Scriptures are unique. In the Hebrew Scriptures there is a prophetic criticism of war and sacrifice (as we will see in the next chapter). Sacks states:

> In general, the Hebrew Bible is hostile to war. The prophets of Israel were the first people in history to see peace as an ideal. Already in the eight century BCE, Isaiah and Micah speak of a time when 'Nation will not take up sword against nations nor will they train for war any more' (Isaiah 2:4; Micah 4:3), and 'They will neither harm nor destroy on all my holy mountain, for the earth will be full of the knowledge of The Lord as the waters cover the sea' (Isaiah 11:9). This is the world's first literature of peace.[27]

King David

King David is revered in Israel's history as their greatest King. He is also acclaimed for ushering in a period of golden splendour in the troubled history of the kingdom of Israel. This is continued through his lineage, and Solomon builds a temple of magnificent grandeur, and produces a body of writings that are unparalleled in the ancient world. And yet, David is a deeply problematic character, and there are clear ethical challenges when it comes to holding him up as one of the greatest kings ancient Israel had ever known.

Some may immediately think that I am about to refer to his idolatry with Bathsheba, and how he subsequently arranges the death of her husband by sending him to the front line. But it is not this episode which I find the most

---

[27] Jonathan Sacks, *The Great Partnership: God, Science and the Search for Meaning* (London: Hodder & Stoughton, 2011), 253.

disturbing, after all, the context those days was one of polygamy, and it would have been very normal for a king to surround himself with a hareem. Of course, arranging to have the husband killed is a more serious matter, but at least he does repent, and wrote one of the most beautiful psalms ever written, Psalm 51, which has stood through history as a reminder of the depths humans can sink to, but also the way back to a place of reconciliation through confession and taking responsibility.[28] But because of David's public confession and contrite response when confronted by the prophet Nathan, this is not the most disturbing episode in David's life (and I am not for one moment playing down the fate of the poor husband). There is a far more odious episode in his life, which incidentally I have rarely heard read at church, let alone sung by a praise band whilst strumming on a guitar. I am referring to 2 Samuel chapter 5.

In 2 Samuel 5:6 shortly after David is anointed king of Israel there is a disturbing passage where it appears that instruction is given of how to defeat the city by attacking the most vulnerable. It reads as follows:

The king and his men marched to Jerusalem against the Jebusites, the inhabitants of the land, who said to David, 'You will not come in here, even the blind and the lame will turn you back'—thinking, 'David cannot come in here'. Nevertheless, David took the stronghold of Zion, which is now the city of David. David had said on that day, 'Whoever wishes to strike the Jebusites, let him get up the water shaft to attack the lame and the blind, those whom David hates'. Therefore it is said, 'The blind and the lame shall not come into the house'. David

---

[28] Psalm 51: Create in Me a Clean Heart, O God
To the choirmaster. A Psalm of David, when Nathan the prophet went to him, after he had gone in to Bathsheba.

occupied the stronghold, and named it the city of David. David built the city all around from the Millo inwards. And David became greater and greater, for the LORD God of hosts, was with him.

The contrast with the picture in the New Testament, where Christ is depicted amongst the poor and the blind, healing them and calling them blessed, could not be more different. In this passage of 2 Samuel the editors/redactors/authors of the day have no ethical dilemma in foregrounding the benefits of a military campaign based on the attack and dehumanisation of the most vulnerable and weak. And then verse 10, where the greatness of King David is extolled, it reminds us that the 'Lord was with him'.

I don't know about you, but I have yet to hear a sermon preached from this passage. I have never seen a children's Bible illustrate this passage, instead they usually focus on David the shepherd boy defeating the giant Goliath, or fending off wild animals to defend his flock. And I am talking about during my conservative upbringing, where 2 Timothy 3:16 used to justify unquestioning literalism ('All Scripture is inspired by God and is useful for teaching, for reproof, for correction, and for training in righteousness, so that everyone who belongs to God may be proficient, equipped for every good work').

How this verse has come to be the foundational text for literalists, is curious, because there is nothing in this verse that states that the text should be interpreted literally and at face value. In fact, I would argue that this text implies something quite different, which holds the key to what we have been discussing in the last few paragraphs, namely the terror passages in the Bible. Could it be that the terror passages, the abuses committed in God's name, the harm unleashed on fellow man in the name of God all feature as part of the canon, not to justify violence in the name of religion, but precisely the opposite: to show us and teach us of the dangers of religious belief when it is used to oppress others? Understating 2 Timothy 3:16 in this context makes sense, because it correctly infers that everything that has been written is useful for teaching, for reproof, for correction.

The Bible is a site of struggle. It holds up a mirror to ourselves, to our propensity to use our religion as a mechanism of oppression rather than of blessing. Our tendency to justify violence in the name of God, rather than loving our neighbour and our enemies, is inferred in many of its most gruesome episodes. The Bible is divinely inspired as it shows us up for who we are, but does not leave us there, but provides a way of overcoming our scapegoating and fears through transforming love.

As Peter Rollins has convincingly argued, the biblical text militates against fundamentalist interpretations by its own very nature, because it doesn't lend itself to one interpretation. The seeds of its own deconstruction are embedded in the text, but this is not to be understood in negative terms, but as liberatory, because it demands that we do not make idols of our particular interpretive framework. It calls us to question our belief that the only valid interpretation is our own, because the biblical text itself militates against this by presenting such a polyphony of voices. Rollins goes to the very heart of what we are considering here:

The biblical text resists such idolatrous readings precisely because it contains so many ideological voices, held together in creative tensions ensuring the impossibility of any final resolution. The result is not an account that is hopelessly ideological, but rather a text that shows the extent to which no one ideology or group do ideologies can lay hold of the divine the text is not only full of fractures, tensions and contradictions but informs us that fractures, tensions and contradictions are all we can hope for [in the here and now].[29]

In this sense, the Bible is very different to the Qur'an, because the Bible is a polyphony of voices, at times competing with each other, reaffirming each other, challenging and evolving; whereas the Qur'an is understood to have been received as divine dictation. It is interesting to note that Christians on the far end of the fundamentalist Richter scale make similar claims about the Bible as some Muslims do about the Qur'an.

But, as I mentioned earlier, those of us who claimed to be the guardians of biblical inerrancy, did not actually follow through with our claims. When we encountered a difficult terror passage, more often than not, we moved on. We too approached the Bible as though it were a pick and mix sweets display we see in every motorway service station or cinema forecourt. And there were good ethical reasons for doing so. But, at the same time we criticised the so-called 'liberals' for not really believing the Bible, for not really taking it for what it is, and what it means. And in case you think that we only did this with difficult Old Testament passages, think again. What about the words of Jesus to the young rich ruler in Mark 10:17-27 when he tells him to sell all he has and give it to the poor? In our comfortable western world we never preached this, for some reason we never took this verse literally (and in the main, we still don't), but we did preach the hell fire damnation message at the end of Matthew 25, and took most of Jesus's mentions of hell at face value. So clearly this model of reading the Bible is deficient, and we need a different approach, a different framework.

Getting back to the 2 Samuel 5 passage, it is important to introduce another passage relating to David as well. I

---

[29] Peter Rollins, *How (Not) To Speak of God* (London: SPCK, 2006), 13.

am grateful for this insight to my friend Louis Bezuidenhout, who I would visit during the bleak Scottish winters to discuss theology. We would sit in his Victorian manse on the banks of Loch Fyne, drinking copious amounts of tea as the rain battered against the window, and discuss books we had recently read. As a Hebrew scholar, a deep thinker and minister in the Church of Scotland, I learnt a lot from him.

I was discussing the disturbing passage (quoted in full above) of 2 Samuel 5, which we have just read, and Louis reminded me of a verse only a couple of chapters later, where David takes in Mephibosheth (Jonathan's son) who was crippled. The full story is recounted in 2 Samuel chapter 9. Look at verse 3 onwards, because it shows how Mephibosheth, despite being cripple, is invited in to the Kings household:

The king said, 'Is there not anyone of the house of Saul, to whom I may show the kindness of God?' Ziba said to the king, 'There remains a son of Jonathan; he is crippled in his feet'. 'Where is he?' Ziba said to the king, 'He is in the house of Machir son of Ammiel, at Lo-debar'. Then King David sent and brought him from the house of Machir the son of Ammiel, at Lo-debar. (2 Samuel 9:3-5)

Only a few chapters on from the passage where David commands an attack on the city by targeting the lame and the crippled, we find him welcoming a crippled man into his household:

Mephibosheth ate at David's table, like one of the king's sons. And Mephibosheth had a young son, whose name was Mica. And all who lived in Ziba's house became Mephibosheth's servants. Mephibosheth lived in Jerusalem, for he always ate always at the king's table. Now he was lame in both his feet. (2 Samuel 9:11-13)

The point my friend Louis was making, is that in the Old Testament, we are   presented with two passages that show radically different types of ethical frameworks. There is seldom any commentary on the passages, but instead they are just presented. We as readers then wrestle with them, and rightly make ethical choices about how we deploy them. As Karen Armstrong states, the way in which interpreters of the biblical texts held these tensions together when reading scripture, was to read them against the principle of love/charity:

> Some of the most important biblical authorities insisted that charity must be the guiding principle of exegesis: any interpretation that spread hatred or disdain was illegitimate. All the world faiths claim that compassion is not only the prime virtue and the test of true religiosity but that it actually introduces us to Nirvana, God the Dao. But sadly the biography of the Bible represents the failures as well as the triumphs of the religious quest. The biblical authors and their interpreters have all too often succumbed to the violence, unkindness and exclusivity that is rife in their societies.[30]

As readers and practitioners of the biblical texts, we have an ethical duty to wrestle with them, not to take them at face value, but to allow them to read us, read our world, and to delve deep within its layers of meanings, always asking, what we can learn from it. Trying to justify Exodus 32 or 2 Samuel 5 is not what the foundation of biblical exegesis should be about. Indeed, to do so would be ethically irresponsible and morally wrong. We need to read these passages in context, and also read the passages which challenge and call the kind of behaviour exhibited in these passages into question.

---

[30] Karen Armstrong, *The Bible: The Biography* (London: Atlantic Books, 2007), 5.

Most scholarship agrees that the books of Samuel (although originally it was one book and only divided in two much later) was written and edited around 630-550 BCE. It is theological history, and as such needs to be understood within the wider literary and socio-political context in which it was written. The literary world of that time was dominated by Homer's *Iliad* and *The Odyssey*, believed to have been written between the 8th and 7th century BCE. The *Iliad* is a piece of epic poetry which narrates the ten year Trojan War and the siege of Troy. The *Odyssey* is a sequel to the *Iliad*, and narrates Odysseus (a.k.a.Ulysses) return home after the war. The reason I mention this in the context of 2 Samuel, is that Ancient Greek mythology of the time is obsessed with war, and the role of the gods in determining certain outcomes. In the *Iliad* there is much talk of the wrath of the gods, the gods commanding war and determining the outcome. Look at the very opening lines of the *Iliad* and you will immediately pick up on these themes:

Sing, goddess, the wrath of Achilles Peleus' son, the ruinous wrath that brought in the Achaians woes innumerable, and hurled down into Hades many strong souls of heroes, and gave their bodies to be prey to dogs and all winged fowls; and so the counsel of Zeus wrought out its accomplishment from the day when forts stride parted Astreides king of men an noble Achilles.

Who then among the gods set the twain at strife and variance? Even the son of Leto and of Zeus; for he in anger at the king sent a sore plague upon the host, that the folk began to perish, because Astreides had done dishonour to Chryses the priest.[31]

The gods who were respected were the warrior gods who won battles, the gods who determined outcomes, in the custom of sending plagues when their honour had been questioned, and displaying wrath and anger as central characteristics. This was the prevalent world view

---

[31] Homer, *The Iliad* (Ware: Hertfordshire, 1995), 1.

of the 8th century BCE, and it is into this context that much of the Old Testament was written down and edited.

We have just touched on a few examples in this chapter on heroes or the Old Testament, which the Jewish and Christian tradition have eulogised and extolled, by emphasising parts of their characteristics whilst ignoring others. But the biblical text does not really allow us to do that. As Peter Rollins has argued, if you take the entirety of the text seriously, it deconstructs itself. That is, it presents different pictures of Moses, Joshua, David etc, which problematises and militates against fixed identities. In one sense, what is going on is that within these characters is something more complex. Within each character there is a struggle. It is as if the powers of good and evil are operating, for at times they are capable of acts of compassion and righteousness; whilst at other times they do not hesitate to carry out murder, genocide, and extreme cruelty when they believe that it is mandated by God.

But unlike the Greek mythical heroes, there is a recurrent strand running through all the Old Testament narratives of repentance and contrition. I am not arguing that this is completely absent in Greek mythology: in the *Iliad* some of the most beautiful poetry is when Achilles shows Priam compassion; but it is not a recurring theme.

We have already briefly touched on psalm 51 of David, where he shows repentance. We also know that David is not allowed to build the Temple because he has shed too much blood. The passage which details this is 1 Chronicles 22:6-8:

Then he called for his son Solomon and charged him to build a house for the LORD, the God of Israel. David said to Solomon, 'My son, I had planned to build a house to the name of the LORD my God. But the word of the LORD came to me, saying, 'You have shed much blood and have waged great wars; you shall not build a house to my name, because you have shed so much blood in my sight on the earth'.

Hang on a minute! Here we have God prohibiting David from building the temple because of the violence and bloodshed he had committed, and the responsibility is thus handed over to Solomon; but throughout the books of Samuel we see David winning battles over his enemies and destroying thousands of enemy soldiers with apparent the blessing (and responding to the apparent will) of God! Throughout the books of Joshua, Deuteronomy, Judges, Samuel etc God is depicted as commanding violence and destruction, whereas in this passage, there is a clear denunciation of it. Why would God punish David by not allowing him to build his temple, if he had commanded him to do violence in the first place? It makes no sense.

It is contradictory if you read all of this at face value. But if you acknowledge that there are a polyphony and multiplicity of voices within the biblical texts, then it begins to make clearer sense. If, as Caputo has argued, the name of God harbours an 'event' rather than an easily identifiable character, then we can begin to engage with these texts in a different way.

As we have seen before, what happens in the Bible is that (when we engage with the entirety of the text), violence and the condemnation of violence are presented alongside each other. What will win out? What will have the final word? Which of the two will be embodied by the incarnate God?

We need to engage with our reading practices in an ethical way that seeks for a hermeneutics that prioritises love, justice, compassion and repentance; over blood lust, violence and retaliation. This leads me to the next chapter, on the significance of the death of Christ.

Chapter 3

Appeasement God

In this chapter I want to examine why Jesus was crucified. To do so I will start out by stating what I was brought up to believe. I will then outline how I have departed from the theology of my youth, to arrive at a very different place.

As I have intimated in previous chapters, I was brought up with a conservative brand of Christianity which assumed 'penal substitution' was the only way in which to understand Christ's atoning work on the Cross. It went something like this: God had created the world to be 'perfect' where there was no sin. But Adam and Eve ate of the forbidden fruit, bringing sin and death into the world. Every human being thereafter was 'born under sin', and therefore condemned to eternal punishment in hell if they did not repent. God hates sin, and because he is holy, he needs to punish it, but instead of punishing us, he sends his son as a perfect sacrifice for sin. Christ dies on the cross in our place, to absorb the righteous wrath of God, and for those of us who accept him, go free. Our sin is exchanged for his righteousness. Eternal torment in hell is exchanged for eternal life in heaven.

Although I do not see it this way now, let me be absolutely clear about one thing. Namely, that I have sat under preachers who have proclaimed this view of atonement and been deeply stirred by the love of God, and transformed by the message of hope. Many of my friends, theologians and ministers whom I love and respect hold firm to the view that penal substitutionary atonement is the central core of all Christian teaching. I respect that. I know that this version of the gospel has power and appeal, and that contrary to some of the ways in which it has been caricatured, it still (as John Stott and others have argued) starts with the love of God. Put simply and paraphrasing Stott's well known argument: it is not because of Christ's sacrifice that God loves us, but the other way round. But rather, because God loves us, he sends his son to become the sin bearer upon whom his holy wrath is poured out. Divine satisfaction is made, and those who accept what Christ has done go free, whilst those who reject his sacrifice are condemned to eternal damnation in the unquenchable fires of hell.

For most of my Christian life I have understood the cross in this way. I have read the Bible through this lens, and some years ago would have considered it sacrilegious to even question this view of atonement. Having said that, always deep within me I have been uncomfortable with the idea that in order to forgive God needs a blood sacrifice. As Brian McClaren has said on numerous occasions (and I paraphrase), it places violence at the very heart of the Christian religion. It sacralises violence. It also puts God in a league with a pantheon of ancient gods or mythology, all of whom demanded sacrifices to appease their anger, be it animal, vegetable or human.

One of the problems with penal substitution is that it hardly differentiates God from other deities, and when you actually de-mythologise what is happening, it is effectively human torture mandated by God to appease his anger (wrath). It takes responsibility away from the Roman soldiers who crucified him and from those who rejected him and were content to collaborate with their imperial masters. Of course, I can already hear in my head comments of outrage from some of my conservative Christian friends who would take issue with what I have just suggested and would argue that it wasn't God's anger that motivated him but his justice. They would probably quote Anselm at me, and talk about the fact that given the seriousness of sin, a high price had to be paid, and they would argue that the fact that God ordained it (many believe before the world began) does not take responsibility away from the human agents who carried it out. They would simply point to the fact that God uses situations even when human beings are sinning and in rejection of Him, and uses these precise situations to bring about his plans and his glory.

I understand all of these objections. In my youth I would deploy them against anyone who doubted the goodness of God. But I am simply not convinced by these arguments anymore. When you strip away everything, you cannot avoid the disturbing notion that the only way God can forgive the human race, is by his son being brutally tortured to death. My conservative Christian friends would say that what is actually going on is that God himself (incarnated in the Son) takes upon himself the wrath, so it is less about an angry God up there gazing down at his suffering Son down here, but united in suffering because of the Trinitarian relationship.

The problem is that however we dress it up and try to rationalise it, we cannot get away from the disturbing truth that God can only forgive through 'redemptive' violence.

The belief in violent blood sacrifices as a means of gaining favour with the gods has a long history, and even today we hear of stories where rituals involving child sacrifice are performed. Let me be clear: I am not comparing this with views of penal substitution, which would be a gross distortion, I am simply stating the fact that blood sacrifices to appease the gods is not unique to Judeo Christianity.

Witch doctors today in Uganda (I use Uganda as an example but could have used other countries) still perform animal sacrifices to appease the Spirits, but there have been multiple cases of children being abducted from the streets of the capital city Kampala, to be used as human sacrifices, when animals were not deemed a good enough sacrifice to appease the spirits. The mutilated bodies of children have been found in the streets of Kampala, abducted and tortured because of a belief that sacrificing them will bring benefits to the community (both material and spiritual). For anyone who doubts this, there are countless reports and articles in the media. One such article was written by BBC correspondent Chris Rogers, entitled 'Where Child Sacrifice is a Business', published on the 11th of October 2011. In it he states:

> School children are closely watched by teachers and parents as they make their way home from school. In playgrounds and on the roadside are posters warning of the danger of abduction by witch doctors for the purpose of child sacrifice [...] The mutilated bodies of children have been discovered at roadsides, the victims of an apparently growing belief in the power of human sacrifice.[32]

I know that some of my Christians friends would accuse me of blasphemy for mentioning penal substitution and child sacrifice (which incidentally was prohibited in the Old Testament) in the same breath. They would argue that God gives of himself by offering up his son. But however you dress it up, there is no getting away from the central idea that salvation and forgiveness can only come through human/divine sacrifice.

On Thursday the 16th of June 2005 the BBC published an article entitled 'Boys Used for Human Sacrifice', which chillingly started off by claiming that 'Children are being

---

[32] Chris Rogers, 'Where Child Sacrifice is a Business', (BBC News Africa, 11th of October 2011). http://www.bbc.co.uk/news/world-Africa-15255357#story_continues_1 (Accessed on 22.10.2014).

trafficked in to the UK from Africa and used for human sacrifices, a confidential report for the for the Metropolitan Police suggests'.[33] In this article it states that certain 'pastors' had labelled some children as witches, with the consequence that these children had been beaten to death, in an attempt to beat the devil out of them. Those questioned about it had said that 'for spells to be powerful it required a sacrifice of a male child unblemished by circumcision'.

What these articles remind us of is that the idea that the spiritual world/deities can be appeased through human sacrifice is still around today. Let me be clear, I am not suggesting for a moment that the brutality and evil of the examples cited above is in anyway comparable to penal substitutionary understandings of atonement, and I know that my friends who still hold to this view would argue that Christ goes to the cross voluntarily, knowing that it is the Father's will and the means through which the penalty of sin can be paid for and gods wrath 'satisfied'. However, there is no getting away from the uncomfortable fact this view basically states that forgiveness, new beginnings, and a right relationship with God can only come once God's anger and wrath has been poured out on his son. He can only be appeased by human/divine sacrifice.

Human/divine sacrifice has a long history as we know. Practically every ancient society practised sacrifice of some sort, whether of animals or produce from the land, and some practised (and continue to) human sacrifice. Sacrificial rituals of animal sacrifice and libations are described in Homer's Odyssey, and Odysseus offered a sacrifice to Zeus before embarking for Troy.

---

[33] http://news.bbc.co.uk/1/hi/uk/4098172.stm (Accessed on 22.10.2014)

Most anthropologists would argue that animal sacrifice originated from hunter-gatherer communities, over 50 thousand years ago during the Upper Palaeolithic era. The reasons were varied, but usually included the idea of offering a libation to the gods, giving back something of value as a gift to the gods which would ensure favour, which was closely related to the idea of appeasing the gods. Human sacrifice evolved out of this context, when it was deemed that something of more value had to be offered to the gods to appease them. In Homer's *Odyssey* Agamemnon sacrifices his daughter Iphigenia because he believes it will bring him success in the Trojan War. When the Aztecs consecrated the pyramid of Tenochtitlan, it is believed that between 10,000 and 80,000 people were sacrificed, as offerings to the gods.[34]

The higher value and status of the sacrifice, the more effective it was. There is a clear parallel here with the understanding of Christ's sacrifice as being the 'perfect' sacrifice that will atone for sin, where the blood of animals is deemed to be ineffective. Hebrews 10:4 is a well-known verse which reads 'For it is impossible for the blood of bulls and goats to take away sins'. Ephesians 2:13 talks about us being 'brought near by the blood of Christ'. Whilst this is traditionally interpreted as proof of penal substitution, it can, of course, be understood in a completely different way: God's incarnation into human form means that he identifies and is at one with his suffering creation. Christ's crucifixion and death at the hands of the Roman soldiers and angry mob, means that he is not exempt from false accusations, torture and death. In this sense his suffering (blood is used as a synecdoche here) brings him close to us, and his resurrection gives us the hope that love will conquer over death.

---

[34] For more information on this see Ross Hassig, 'El sacrificio y las guerras floridas', *Arqueología Mexicana* Vol XI, no. 63 (2003), 46-51.

James Frazer devotes a whole section of his book *The Golden Bough* to human and divine sacrifice, and the notion of 'transference of evil' through a scapegoat figure. This idea was around long before Judeo-Christianity took it up. Practically every ancient tribe/people practised sacrifice in some form. Frazer reminds us that:

Among the Semites of Western Asia the king, in a time of national danger, sometimes gave his own son to die as a sacrifice for the people. Thus Philo of Byblus, in his work on the Jews, says: 'It was an ancient custom in a crisis of great danger that the ruler of a city or nation should give his beloved son to die for the whole people, as a ransom offered to the avenging demons; and the children thus offered were slain with mystic rites. So Cronus, whom the Phoenicians call Israel, being king of the land and having an only-begotten son called Jeoud (for in the Phoenician tongue Jehoud signifies 'only begotten'), dressed him in royal robes and sacrificed him upon an altar in time of war when the country was in great danger from the enemy. When the king of Moab was besieged by the Israelites and hard beset, he took his eldest son, who should have reigned in his stead, and offered him for a burnt offering on the wall.

But among the Semites the practice of sacrificing their children was not confined to kings. In times of great calamity, such as pestilence, drought, or defeat in war, the Phoenicians used to sacrifice one of their dearest to Baal.[35]

Frazer goes on to argue that the Israelites absorbed many of their ideas about sacrifice from 'among the Canaanites, or aboriginal inhabitants of Palestine, whom the invading Israelites conquered but did not exterminate'.[36] Frazer crucially reminds us that Yahweh utterly condemns these practices, and prohibits the children of Israel from engaging in child sacrifice, citing

---

[35] James George Frazer, *The Golden Bough: A Study in Magic and Religion*, edited by Robert Frazer (Oxford: Oxford U.P., 1994), 265-266.
[36] Frazer, *The Golden Bough*, 266.

Deuteronomy 18:9-12, which reads 'When you come into the land that the LORD your God is giving you, you must not learn to imitate the abhorrent practices of those nations. No one shall be found among you who makes a son or daughter pass through the fire, or who practices divination, or is a soothsayer, or an augur, or a sorcerer, or one who casts spells, or who consults ghosts of spirits, or who seeks oracles from the dead. For whoever does these things is abhorrent to The Lord; it is because of such abhorrent practices that The Lord your God us driving then out before you'.

Frazer uses this critique of human sacrifice as recorded in Deuteronomy 18 to remind us about the pervasiveness of sacrifice in the prevailing cultures of the day, and the mandate of Yahweh to be different. Frazer then asks what in my view is a key question:

It would be interesting, though it might be fruitless, to enquire how far the Hebrew prophets and psalmists were right in their opinion that the Israelites learned these and other gloomy superstitions only through contact with the old inhabitants of the land, that the primitive purity of faith and morals which they brought with them from the free air of the desert was tainted and polluted by the grossness and corruption of the heathen in the day land of Canaan.[37]

Frazer's tone is in keeping with the time when he was writing, in the latter part of the 19th century and beginning of the 20th, but his observation is an important one, because it raises the question about the permeability and syncretism of the ancient religion of the Children of Israel, and the dialogic tension within the Bible between voices which demand sacrifice and voices which denounce it. Could it be that the end of sacrificial rituals brought about by the death of Christ resonates with the voices in the Old

---

[37] Frazer, *The Golden Bough*, 267.

Testament which question the value of sacrifice, and firmly denounce human sacrifice? Could it be that we are to understand the Bible as a site of struggle, a record of how the children of Israel understood God, and for the way in which God made himself known to them? But the one who was the great unknown, whose face could not be revealed, unlike the material and visible golden calves and other gods, could not be reduced to the images they projected of him?

We want to visualise God, just as they did back then. We want to see God. But throughout the Old Testament we are reminded that God is the one who cannot be seen. In Exodus 33:18-23 there is an exchange between Moses and Yahweh. Moses wants to see God, and asks him in verse 18 to show him his glory, and God replies by saying that 'I will make my goodness pass before you, and will proclaim before you the name THE LORD., and I will be gracious to whom I will be gracious, and will show mercy on whom I will show mercy. But he said, 'you cannot see my face, for no one shall see me and live'. The passage then describes how God makes a compromise with Moses, telling him to stand in the cleft of a rock, where he 'will cover him with his hand' until he has passed by, and then once he has passed by he will remove his hand and Moses will be able to see his back, but not his face.

Yahweh was differentiating himself from the other tangible, visible gods of gold and silver. The children of Israel, no different to us today in that regard, wanted to domesticate God, reduce him to a recognisable face; but that is never a possibility in the Old Testament writings. This contrasted with the other gods, who were materialised in stone, wood and precious metals, satisfying their followers' desire for tangible and recognisable traits. But Yahweh will have none of it, he will be known only by showing 'making his goodness pass before him' as it says in verse 19, and by showing his grace and mercy on whom he will, as stated in verse 20.

True faith calls us to believe even when we cannot see. Just as the photographer of old enters the darkened room to reveal his picture, he must trust that the process will work, and that the true image will be revealed. The camera obscura works by light entering darkness, and from that an image begins to emerge.

Like the children of Israel, we too want to explain God, to have a picture of what she is really like, and like the children of Israel, we can worship a particular image of what we think God is like. For the children of Israel that could take on many forms: the warrior God who helped them win battles, the lover-God who is jealous for their devotion, the merciful God who leads them out of slavery, the judge who will bring justice and destroy their enemies (their greatest fears). And in a way, we are no different today. We want a God who will sort out our world, who will take away our problems, who will banish away our greatest fears; and so we construct her as such, and the images we carry of her in our minds can be seen as a kind of idolatry. We need to be reminded that she is the God who cannot be reduced and easily contained in our understanding, but she is the wild, free and unknowable God, who moved upon the waters of chaos at the beginning of time, bringing life out of the chaotic depths. She is a God who disrupts our comfortable images of her, which is why she can only be known through faith, which enables us to believe even though we cannot see her, to trust even when we are consumed with doubt, to believe that she is at work in our world, despite the fact that God seems absent for most of the time in a world of so much suffering and pain. This fits in with the New Testament as well. Throughout the synoptic gospels (and most notably in Mark) there is what is known in theological circles as 'the messianic secret'. Jesus tells them to tell no one about who he is, he heals and performs miracles and tells those he has healed to not tell anyone. He doesn't want to be known by one aspect of his ministry. He doesn't want to be reduced to one image in their minds, either as healer, or story-teller, or rabbi. The God who veils himself in the Old Testament (in the passage in Exodus which we have just read God veils Moses's eyes so that he cannot see his face). In the New Testament the veil in the temple is only ripped open when Jesus is crucified. This seems to suggest that it is only through the actions of God, his work and evidence in our midst, that he can be known. The veil is ripped when Jesus shows love and forgiveness to his persecutors and accusers, revealing to us a new manifestation of what God is really like, that goes far beyond what we could ever imagine or dream of. It shatters our reductive images which try to domesticate God, open up (similar to the latter half of Exodus 33) a new way of living which involves standing up to injustice non-violently and refusing to see those who persecute us and defame us as enemies. And it is in this way that God is truly revealed and seen. This is so much more powerful than an image we may have of her. For God is love. God is love in action. We often sing the short refrain 'ubi caritas et amor. Ubi caritas, Deus ibi est', which means where there is love, God is.

It is Jesus' non-violence and love in the face of torture and derision that shows us the transforming love of God. These attributes show us what God is truly like. For Christ goes to that place of death and darkness, where in a sense, all the evil and hatred and rejection from down the centuries is thrown at him, and in responding in love he shows us a better way, the way of God. Timothy Radcliffe puts it like this:

Jesus' sacrifice upon the altar of the cross was not one more bloody example of this sacred violence but its defeat. He shows it up as empty and futile. 'It is impossible that the blood of bulls and goats should take away sins' (Hebrews 10.4). Jesus' death was a massive rejection of a whole way of being religious. One can also see it as a culmination of a long and gradual process by which our Jewish ancestors withdrew from sacred violence [...]

[...] But this innocent and forgiving victim will transform that hate-filled unity into the communion of the kingdom: 'I, when I am lifted up, will draw all to myself' (John 12.32). This is Jesus' costly sacrifice. It is not endured to propitiate an angry God, but so as to take upon himself all the vengeance and blood lust of humanity. This is the fulfilment of Isaiah's vision of the suffering servant: 'Surely he has borne our griefs and carried our sorrows, yet we esteemed him stricken, smitten by God, and afflicted. But he was wounded for our transgressions, he was bruised for our iniquities; upon him was the chastisement that made us whose and with his stripes we are healed' (Isaiah 53.4). We esteemed him smitten by God, but we were wrong. It is we who smote him and his forgiveness will transform the lynch mob into the communion of the church.[38]

Throughout his book (which I highly recommend) Radcliffe reminds us of how the Judeo Christian God is differentiated from gods who practice violence. I can hear some of you saying but that simply cannot be true when we read the Bible, for on numerous occasions God is depicted as a warrior god and a God who destroys and commands his people to kill their enemies. And what about the concept of hell, where God not only destroys his enemies, but keeps them alive in perpetual torture with no relief, which is worse than any torture which human beings can inflict on each other?

There is no question that some of the writers and redactors of the Bible had a view of God that was violent

---

[38] Timothy Radcliffe, *Why Go to Church: The Drama of the Eucharist* (London & New York: Continuum, 2009), 119, 121-122.

and bent on retribution. This is hardly surprising, given the religious world-view of the time. But that image of God is progressively questioned and problematised, and it does not have the final word. What interests me are the processes of revelation and evolution. Revelation is not so much progressive, but multi-layered. There are moments of real epiphany in the Old Testament, such as the command to welcome the stranger and the prohibition to kill, which trump the other depictions of God because they are later confirmed by Christ himself.

Timothy Radcliffe is one of many theologians (Catherine Keller is another) who reminds us that the creation account evoked in Genesis is not a violent act. Timothy Radcliffe argues:

Nearly all the myths of their neighbours understood creation as a violent act, the destruction of some monster which embodied the waters of chaos. For example, in the Babylonian epic of creation, the Enuma Elish, Marduk, the storm god, slaughters Tiamat, the goddess of the sea, to make the universe. We can see vestiges of this violent creation in the Old Testament, as when Isaiah looks to the day when 'the Lord with his hard and great and strong sword will punish Leviathan the fleeing serpent, Leviathan the twisting serpent, and he will slay the dragon that is in the sea' (Isaiah 27.1). But in Genesis, no one gets killed to make the world. The Spirit hovers over the formless void. God speaks a word and everything comes to be. Creation *ex nihilo* is a step towards a religion without violence. And in the Old Testament we could plot, if we had the space, the growing hesitation about the whole sacrificial system: 'For I desire steadfast love and not sacrifice, the knowledge of God, rather than burnt offerings' (Hosea 6.6).[39]

The creation account in Genesis depicts the spirit of God hovering over the waters, bringing created order out of chaos. I will address later why a seemingly good and yet

---

[39]Timothy Radcliffe, *Why Go to Church,* 119-120.

'all powerful' God can allow evil, but some would argue that the first creative act of God was to bring light. That God is part of the process of bringing life and created order out of chaos, bringing it to its full completion through the processes and cycles of life, death, decay and rebirth, seems to be suggested by a re-reading of the Genesis account. This view calls into question the traditional 'all powerful' God who creates 'ex nihilo'. We will consider this and aspects of what is known as 'process theology' in the next two chapters. This slight departure from the theme of atonement is not altogether unrelated, as those who support a penal substitutionary view of atonement would for the most part, reject process theology. Instead, they would believe (as I was brought up to believe for many years) that before the foundation of the earth God knew that he would create humankind and that it would 'fall', and that to appease his anger he would need to send a flood and wipe out most of humanity except for one family and a sample of animals, and then much later (in order to appease his anger again), he would require a perfect blood sacrifice (his son). However, this sacrifice would not save the entire human race, only those who believed, the remaining 90 % (let's be generous here) would be condemned to eternal torture in hell. This form of torture would be far worse than anything Hitler, Pol Pot, Stalin, or Isis could inflict, because there would be no end to it. Humans would be kept alive eternally to ensure that the torture never ends.

It is the fantasy of a psychopath, a mass murderer, a merciless torturer, and it is incredible that it has held currency in Christian belief for so long, as it paints a picture of God that is truly barbaric. Those defending it would argue that it represents justice and how seriously God takes sin etc.

But when you think this through, it makes no sense, for punishing someone by condemning them to eternal torture is hardly justice. Let's call it by its name and recognise that it is barbaric torture of the worst kind. This is not the place to go into the issue of eternal damnation, just to say that the belief in eternal damnation and penal substitution go hand in hand, and those who support one usually firmly believe the other.

I came to a point in my life (actually when I was leading a discussion table at an Alpha course which the church I was involved in was hosting) when I actually came to a serious road block in my faith. It was through hearing 'the gospel' message Alpha talk, preached by a sincere and loving member of the leadership team with the best of intentions. But it just did not make any sense to me. It wasn't just that it made no sense, but it implicitly portrayed God as a manipulative tyrant, who gets so angry about the world he has created, that he has to calm himself down through blood sacrifice, and that somehow this loving God could be worshiped, even though those who were 'unfortunate' enough to be born into a different religion, or those who for whatever reason did not believe, would face an eternity of unrelenting torture.

I could not worship this kind of a God any longer. And whilst I am not critiquing the Alpha course, reading through the prescribed book by Nicky Gumbel *Questions of Life: A Practical Introduction to the Christian Faith* left me with more questions than answers. The very act of trying to neatly package the mysteries of life, death, meaning and the Christian faith simply seemed to rob it of its mystery and transcendent beauty. It was from then on that my questioning of all I had been brought up to believe really intensified.

It was soon after that experience that I came across the work of French anthropologist Rene Girard. In his well-known book *Violence and the Sacred* he articulates the theory of 'mimetic violence', which goes something like this. Human beings, from the very beginning, desire what the other has, and this creates conflict. Anyone who has had young children will have seen at first hand a clear example of this. Imagine your child is playing happily in a room full of toys. Your child happens to be playing with a toy train. Another child walks in and picks up a brightly coloured ball which has been lying in the corner and ignored (until now) by your child. But something changes in the atmosphere and the dynamics in the room. Your child now wants the ball. He is not content to play with the toy train anymore, but wants the ball which the other child is playing with. It creates conflict when he goes up and grabs the ball of the other child, and the peaceful nursery room is changed into a site of conflict. This is called 'mimetic desire'. For Girard, it lies at the heart of the human condition and can be found in every society.

But what has this got to do with penal substitution and human/animal sacrifice, you may ask? What Girard argues is that in ancient societies, the way in which conflict was resolved, was by uniting around a scapegoat. Imagine the following scenario. The crops have failed because of a lack of rain one particular year, it is thought that this is a punishment from the god(s). Conflict arises because there is a lack of food. The tribe finds someone to blame. The person may be entirely innocent, but pronouncements are made, rumours run wild that the gods are angry because something he or she has done. The 'community' unites in their anger and direct it at the scapegoat.

The scapegoat is either chased out the community, or put to death, and order is restored. James George Frazer dedicates a whole section of his book on the topic of the scapegoat. In the introductory paragraphs he sets out what he thinks of it as a practice.

Writing as an intellectual in what was the world's imperial super-power of the day, Frazer refers to other cultures in ways that would be unacceptable in our day and age. But this should not detract from the important point he is making about scapegoating:

> The accumulated misfortunes and sins of the whole people are sometimes laid upon the dying god, who is supposed to bear them away for ever, leaving the people innocent and happy. The notion that we can transfer our guilt and sufferings to some other being who will bear them for us is familiar to the savage mind. It arises from a very obvious confusion between the physical and the mental, between the material and the immaterial. Because it is possible to shift a load of wood, stones, or what not, from our own back to the back of another, the savage fancies that it is equally possible to shift the burden of pains and sorrows to another, who will suffer them in his stead. Upon this idea he acts, and the result is an endless number of very un amiable devices for palming off upon someone else the trouble which man shrinks from bearing himself. In short, the principle of vicarious suffering is commonly understood and practiced by races who stand on a low level of social and intellectual culture. In the following pages I shall illustrate the theory and the practice as they are found among the savages in all their naked simplicity, undisguised by the refinements of metaphysics and the subtleties of theology.[40]

In this regard, the Old Testament practice of sending the scape goat out in to the wilderness bearing the sins of the camp certainly marks an improvement from societies who used humans. However, if you believe in penal substitution, then then this will be reversed centuries later, when it is deemed that an animal scapegoat is not good

---

[40] Frazer, *The Golden Bough*, 557.

enough to atone for the sins of humanity and appease God, so the son of God is sent as a perfect sacrifice.

What is so liberating about Rene Girard's writings, is that he argues is that Christianity is unique in that it frees us from the need to scapegoat. It exposes scapegoating for what it is, and Christ shows us a new way. God, in Christ, aligns himself with the victim, by facing execution on the Cross. It is a seminal and transformative moment, in that God not only identifies himself with the victim (in the context of first century Palestine under Roman military occupation this means crucifixion for all who pose a threat to imperial rule), but declares that the victim is innocent. It shifts the balance from a God who demands sacrifice. It boldly states that we should no longer scapegoat, because the scapegoat is innocent. Christ identifies and reveals a God who is not associated with the powerful military leaders who put Jesus to death, but with the marginalised outsider who becomes the victim, as Timothy Radcliffe argues, cited earlier in this chapter. Rene Girard avers in *Violence and the Sacred*: 'Men can dispose of their violence more efficiently if they regard the process not as something emanating from within themselves, but as a necessity imposed from without, a divine decree whose least infraction calls down terrible punishment'.[41] Or in other words: mankind has used God to justify the violence within their own hearts. If God is portrayed as a being who gets angry and inflicts 'terrible punishment', then humankind can justify the violence in its own heart, and project it back onto God. But according to Girard, Christ comes and liberates us from this image of God, and from the violence within our own hearts. In responding non-violently but in forgiveness and love to those who crucify

---

[41] Rene Girard, *Violence and the Sacred* (London: The Athlone Press, 1988), 14.

him, he redeems us from our need to scapegoat and inflict violence.

This truly constitutes what philosopher Slavoj Zizek would call 'an event':

This is an event at its purest and most minimal: something shocking, out of joint, that appears to happen all of a sudden and interrupts the usual flow of things; something that emerges seemingly out of nowhere, without discernible causes, an appearance without solid being as its foundation.

There is, by definition, something 'miraculous' in an event, from the miracles of our daily lives to those of the most sublime spheres, including that of the divine. The eventual nature of Christianity arises from the fact that to be a Christian requires a belief in a singular event--the death and resurrection of Christ.[42]

Zizek's notion of the 'event' applied here to Christianity makes sense at one level to the extent that the crucifixion interrupted 'the flow of things', although in that day, lamentably, the crucifixion of criminals was commonplace and not seen as shocking. Moreover, Jesus' crucifixion does not emerge out of nowhere, there are traceable reasons why he is condemned by the authorities of the day and crucified on a Roman cross. A little further on Zizek goes adds that an event primarily about a new way of seeing and understanding something: 'at its most elementary, event is not something that occurs within the world, but is *a change of the very frame through which we perceived the world and engage in it*'.[43] At one level, the crucifixion of Jesus is not shocking in that Rome crucified so-called criminals and political rebels in the thousands. What is truly remarkable (whether you profess to have Christian

---

[42] Slavoj Zizek, *Event: Philosophy in Transit* (London: Penguin Books, 2014), 2.
[43] Zizek, *Event*, 10.

faith or whether you don't) is the way in which Jesus' death on the cross is singled out from all the other deaths, so much so that the way in which we record and measure history itself in the Gregorian calendar is marked by a before and an after this event. But Zizek's definition of event becomes more useful when we discuss how we interpret the crucifixion, because an event represents '*a change of the very frame through which we perceived the world and engage*'.[44]

As intimated earlier, I grew up believing that there was only one way to interpret Christ's crucifixion. Basically Jesus died on the cross as an atoning sacrifice, taking the punishment that my sins deserved. I now see this very differently, the frame through which I view it has been altered, so much so that the interpretation which informs my Christian faith and my Christian doubt, radically changes the significance of Christ's crucifixion. The problem with viewing the cross through the lens of penal substitution is that it runs the risk of viewing it in isolation of the rest of Christ's life. The atoning, redemptive and saving nature of what Christ represents for us, is reduced to the cross. However, whilst not for one second playing down the implications and central importance of Jesus' crucifixion, I see the very incarnation of God into human flesh as an act that is deeply redemptive and atoning. Redemptive in that it reminds us that we are made in the image of God, which dignifies the human condition and calls upon us to view others as those created in the image of God. It militates against our tendency to dehumanise and scapegoat others. At the same time, God's incarnation in Christ is an atoning work. The etymology of atoning is 'at-one-ment', the idea that God presences himself amongst us by taking up human form, and shows us a new way of being human. This is truly a moment of deep

---

[44] Zizek, *Event*, 10.

transformational value, and event that interrupts the very course of history itself.

Christ's death on the cross represents God going the full way for us. It shows us a God whose love will stop at nothing, whose love will not be compromised, even if he has to pay for it in death. In the laying down of his life non-violently, rebuking Peter for taking up the sword, he shows us a new way of living which is not based on violence and retaliation. It isn't about an angry God up there whose wrath can only be satisfied through the blood sacrifice of his son (although there is no doubt that numerous passages in the Bible suggest that, reflecting the views of how some understood it), but about God Emmanuel down here, at one with his creation, showing that we must respond in love to our accusers, that we are to love our enemies. This is a truly transformative and redeeming act. And in going through death and rising again, it proclaims that death will not have the final word, but love will.

What about the idea that he dies for our sins? I do not believe that Jesus dies to appease an angry God, but, to the alarm of most liberals, I believe that there is a sense in which 'he dies for our sins'. Jesus goes to the place of death, where hatred, rejection, scapegoating and a whole host of other grievances are set upon him by those who accuse him. These human traits are universal, and I recognise them in my own heart, because I too have engaged in scape-goating to avoid taking full responsibility for my actions, I have rejected God in the day to day, by not loving as he loved, I have harboured hatred for others and not loved my enemies as I should. So there is a sense in which the sin of Christ's accusers and tormentors is also my sin. In a sense, it is as though all the sin of humanity is hurled against him, and he absorbs it unto himself, and in responding in love and not violence, cleanses us from our sin, frees us from its grip and power, defeats death and the fear and bondage, descends into the very depths of hell itself showing a way out, and reveals a God who wants to be at one with us, and who calls us back to himself. It is not done to calm down an angry God who will only forgive through blood sacrifice. This would make him no different to practically every deity throughout history, because as we have seen, blood sacrifice has been present in most ancient societies, and our Judaic forebears were no different in this regard. But Christ's crucifixion marks the end of this way of doing religion, because it reveals what God is really like. God is one of us. God is not exempt from suffering, but shows a way through it, and this gives hope and the promise of resurrection and renewal to all the victims of violence and dehumanisation which humanity has witnessed down the centuries. He is the lamb who is slain for us.

Christ lives a life of self-giving love and establishes a kingdom not based on earthly power and coercion but self-emptying. He is not crucified to appease the wrath of an angry God, as had been the case with thousands of human and animal sacrifices down through the ages. In fact, when Jesus overturns the tables of the money lenders in the temple in Matthew 21:12[45], it is a prophetic act which subverts traditional religious practices. That temple trade would have been based around the buying and selling of animals for temple sacrifice. Jesus rejects this way of doing religion, and echoing the prophetic voices of old which had boldly declared that God did not delight in animal sacrifices Isaiah 1:11[46], categorically puts and end a whole

---

[45] 'Then Jesus entered the temple and drove out all who were selling and buying in the temple, and he overturned the tables of the money-changers and the seats of those who sold doves. He said to them, "It is written, 'My house shall be called a house of prayer,' but you are making it a den of robbers."

[46] 'What to me is the multitude of your sacrifices?

system of religious dogma and opens up a new way where the marginalised, the outcasts, those who are victimised and become the scapegoats of society, are the very ones through whom God will establish his kingdom on earth. In fact, further on in that same chapter of Isaiah it places justice and the help of the poor at the heart of religion, not blood sacrifices:

Wash yourselves; make yourselves clean;
remove the evil of your deeds from before my eyes;
cease to do evil,

learn to do good;
seek justice,
rescue the oppressed;
Appeasement God

defend the orphan,
plead for the widow.
  (Isaiah 1:16-17)

This 8th century BCE call to do justice, reject animal sacrifices, and to help the widow is a moment of true epiphany. It is unparalleled and unique when compared to the world literatures of the day, and it is no wonder that Christ was to identify his ministry so closely with Isaiah, in particular with the 'suffering servant' in the second Isaiah. In this context, it is not by coincidence that Jesus will never identify himself with the Old Testament passages of war and ethnic cleansing which we looked at in the previous chapter, but identifies himself with the suffering servant whose main mission is to heal the broken hearted

---

says the LORD;
I have had enough of burnt offerings of rams
and the fat of fed beasts;
I do not delight in the blood of bulls,
or of lambs, or of goats'.

and bind up the wounds of those in this life, in there here and now.[47] The growing emphasis with the

---

[47] Who has believed what we have heard?
And to whom has the arm of the LORD been revealed?
2
For he grew up before him like a young plant,
and like a root out of dry ground;
he had no form or majesty that we should look at him,
nothing in his appearance that we
should desire him.
3
He was despised and rejected by men;
a man of sorrows, and acquainted with infirmity;
and as one from whom others hide their faces
he was despised, and we held him of no account.
4
Surely he has borne our infirmities
and carried our diseases;
yet we accounted him stricken,
struck down by God, and afflicted.
5
But he was wounded for our transgressions;
 crushed for our iniquities;
upon him was the punishment that
made us whole,
and by his bruises we are healed.
6
All we like sheep have gone astray;
we have a turned to our own way;
and the LORD has laid on him
the iniquity of us all.
7
He was oppressed, and he was afflicted,
yet he did not open his mouth;
like a lamb that is led to the slaughter,
and like a sheep that before its shearers is silent,
so he opened not his mouth.
8
By a perversion of justice he was taken away;
Who could have imagined his future?

afterlife was to come much later, as Platonism influenced and shaped Christianity with its stark division between the

---

For he was cut off from the land of the living,
stricken for the transgression of my people.
9
They made his grave with the wicked
and his tomb with the rich,
although he had done no violence,
and there was no deceit in his mouth.
10
Yet it was the will of the LORD to crush him;
with pain.
When you make his life an offering for sin,
he shall see his offspring; he shall prolong his days;
through the will of the LORD shall prosper.
11
Out of his anguish he shall see light;

by his knowledge shall the righteous one, my servant,
Make many to be accounted righteous. (Isaiah 53)
and he shall bear their iniquities.
12
Therefore I will divide him a portion with the many,
and he shall divide the spoil with the strong,
because he poured out his soul to death
and was numbered with the transgressors;
yet he bore the sin of many,
and makes intercession for the transgressors.

spiritual and the material worlds, and its idealisation of the spiritual realm.

The image of God is formed in the camera obscura of life. We begin to glimpse in part, sometimes mistaking the faint outline of the image for the image itself.

We still only see in part. We still do not fully understand the mystery of God. The realisation of this should cause us to hold our own beliefs with humility, for none of us have the whole picture.

Chapter 4

Power God

Since the beginning of time, human beings have been obsessed with power. To have power enables you to fight off other predators. It enables you to protect resources. Throughout the emergence of humans on this planet, those who were able to develop weaponry to give them advantage in battle were those whose tribes flourished at the expense of others. As history progressed nomadic societies began to settle in towns and villages, those occupying strategic locations built fortresses and strongholds to protect against invading predatory enemies.

From the beginnings of time, power and wealth have been inextricably linked. Every world Empire in history has built up its military to protect its territories and resources. From the Greek and Romans to the Ottomans, the Spanish and Portuguese to the Dutch and the British, to the USA, the USSR and China: no imperial enterprise has ever been achieved without the backing of massive military might. In medieval times, royalty and the noble classes were able to accumulate land and fortunes by taking land, and building walled fortresses around it which were protected by small armies (usually comprised and made up of the poor). It created a system that is still largely the same today: namely that it is the poor who swell the armies of the USA and UK, and like in medieval times, they fight to preserve a world structure which favours the rich and the elite (it is just that in the west more and more of us pertain to this class, as, on the whole, we consume more than our fair share of natural resources). As I write this, we are commemorating the 100th anniversary of the start of World War I, arguably one of the most absurd and avoidable wars of all time, and one of the deadliest. What started out as a single act of criminal aggression with the assassination of Arch Duke Ferdinand, ended with a four year mega-war, where all the advances of technology and industry were put to the test, with an estimated toll of human lives amounting to more than 16 million, with a further 20 million who were injured. Of course, the assassination of Arch Duke Ferdinand was not the sole cause of the war, but the trigger for the big imperial powers of the day to expand and consolidate their empires. The 20,000 men who fell in one day of trench warfare in the Battle of the Somme, disproportionately made-up by conscripts from the poorer classes were fighting to preserve a world order which maintained imperial structures that favoured the rich and the powerful, societies from which they were largely excluded. It is hardly surprising that in 1917 Russia underwent a revolution that was to change the course of the 20th century, when conscripts returning from the trenches on the Eastern Front, largely made up of the peasant classes, exhausted and traumatised from witnessing first-hand the slaughter of hundreds of thousands of their fellow comrades to preserve a world order from which they were largely excluded, rose up in rebellion against Tsarist Russia. The rest, as they say, is history.

Let me be clear about one thing: I am not in favour of violent revolution and armed struggle (even if it is to 'liberate' the poor). History shows that more often than not, those who rebel and overturn governments, once they have seized power, often end up as bad (and sometimes worse) than the regimes they have brought down. Violence is never the solution. The Russian Revolution of 1917 and its aftermath is but one example of this. War needs an enemy, and so it always dehumanises the other. Once the enemy is dehumanised, he becomes easier to kill.

It therefore comes as little surprise that in matters such as empire-building, which involve invasion and control, life and death; religion has been invoked, both to seek victory and success on the one hand, and as moral justification for war on the other. Competing human emotions, blood-lust, envy and greed often masquerading behind the thin veneer of religious belief, as a means of justifying it.

As priest and peace activist Father John Dear has explored in his writings, much of our military war machines are built to protect our access to the world's resources. In a global system where the resources are unequally distributed, this can only be done through military might. John Dear reminds us of the injustice of spending so much on arms and weaponry when there are such high levels of hunger and chronic poverty in the world. I quote his words in full because of their relevance to our world today:

We are accustomed to recognising violence when it is inflicted by weapons. But the violence of our world occurs on many levels, from the violence within us, to interpersonal and societal violence, to the global, structural violence of war, nuclear weapons environmental destruction, hunger, sexism, racism, homelessness, abortion, torture, the death penalty and the rampant poverty that leaves over one billion people in misery. Though cancer, AIDS, heart disease, natural disasters and accidents of every variety kill people by the millions each year, the deliberate violence of war and systemic injustice kill human beings at an enormous rate—a plague that humanity has inflicted on itself.

The first level of violence includes the over-arching global, structured injustice which institutionalises the worldwide oppression of poverty, systematically accumulates the world's resources in the hands of a small minority of rich people and forces the vast majority of humanity to suffer starvation, misery and degradation. In recent decades the church has called this systemic injustice 'institutionalised, legalised violence, whether in the form of economic exploitation, political domination, or abuse of military might'. These global systems of economic exploitation and political and military domination, which cause and maintain poverty, override all other forms of violence. Although the United States has only 5 percent of the world's population, it consumes nearly 60 percent of the world's resources. Twenty percent of the world's population controls 80 percent of the world's goods, another twenty percent lives in desperate poverty, and 60 percent just get by. As Ghandi said, 'poverty is the worst form of violence'.

Institutionalised economic injustice is only possible because of the world-wide weapons systems and military forces which wage war and threaten the nuclear destruction of the planet in order to protect this unjust arrangement. Francis of Assisi long ago summed up the link between war and greed. 'If we want to own possessions', he observed, 'we must also have weapons' [...] Because the first-world elite hoards the world's goods, it needs an elaborate and lethal weapons system to protect through violence the goods that it has stolen from the rest of the world [...] As Catholic social teaching has long taught, economic systems and structures which maintain the lifestyle of the first world's wealthy already kill the poor of the worlds as the Second Vatican Council declared, 'The arms race is an utterly treacherous trap for humanity, and one which injures the poor to an intolerable degree'. 'The arms race is to be condemned unreservedly', Paul VI wrote. 'It is *in itself and act of aggression* against those who are the victims of it. It is an act of aggression, which amounts to a crime, for *even when they are not used,* by their cost alone, *armaments kill the poor by causing then to starve'* [italics in original]. In other words, the bomb has already gone off in the world of the poor. Poverty and militarism are inextricably linked.[48]

Why are the majority of Christians today are largely in favour of war? Why is it that we have to turn to the Quaker, Amish and the Mennonite traditions as examples of non-violent resistance? This is not the time and place to go into the issue of 'just war'/non-violence (and those interested in pursuing this further should read the works

---

[48] John Dear, *The God of Peace: Toward a Theology of Nonviolence* (Eugene: Wipf and Stock Publishers, 2005), 5-7.

of John Dear), but it is important to reference (albeit briefly) as we consider issues of power in the context of the Christian religion. Power and violence (as we have seen in chapter 2) have all too often been historical bedfellows (both within religion and world history at large). Christ's crucifixion breaks this association, for it shows a God whose power is manifested through weakness, not a God who comes down and crushes the Roman Empire through force (as would have been expected by many of the Old Testament prophets), but one who subverts it from within through love. We will go on to explore this idea in more depth in the following chapter, so I am referencing it now briefly so that we can bear it in mind as we consider the ways in which the Christian religion has been obsessed with power.

One of the chapters in the New Testament which has been misused and misunderstood by many is Acts 1:6-8, which reads: 'So when they had come together, they asked him, "Lord, is this the time when you will restore the kingdom to Israel?" He replied, "It is not for you to know times or periods that the Father has set by his own authority. But you will receive power when the Holy Spirit has come upon you, and you will be my witnesses in Jerusalem, in all Judea and Samaria, and to the ends of the earth.'

I have heard these verses read out in many a charismatic meeting, where members of the congregation have whipped themselves into a frenzy over this verse, and have interpreted as the guarantee of power to have all their financial, health and life problems sorted (a kind of American dream of wealth, health and success masqueraded as 'spirit filled' Christianity). But this has nothing to do with the text in question, or indeed the context in which it was written down. The evidence of the Holy Spirit is to make us more like Christ. The evidence of the Holy Spirit is not seen by people writhing around the floor in ecstasy and making animal noises (I am referring to some of common features around following the so-called Toronto Blessing that emerged in 1994 at The Toronto Airport Vinyard Church, and more recently Lakeland Revival headed by someone who claimed he had met the apostle Paul, and who conversed with an Angel by the name of Emma who showed him a vision of gold coins as proof that he would become very rich).

I am always alarmed when the gospel gets twisted into a prosperity message of wealth, health and success, which does not transform the world or call for an end to structures of economic injustice that keep so many in poverty. The evidence of the Spirit is not to be measured in material wealth. Scripture is very clear that the evidence of the Holy Spirit is the fruit, as mentioned in Galatians 5:22, which reads 'The fruit of the Spirit is love, joy, peace, patience, kindness, goodness, faithfulness,gentleness, and self-control. There is no law against such things'.

In Matthew chapter 7:15-20 we are reminded that it is by their fruits that we are to know whether they are a true or false prophet: 'Beware of false prophets, who come to you in sheep's clothing but inwardly are ravenous wolves. You will know them by their fruits. Are grapes gathered from thorns, or figs from thistles? In the same way, every good tree bears good fruit, but the bad tree bears bad fruit. A good tree cannot bear bad fruit, nor can a bad tree bear good fruit. Every tree that does not bear good fruit is cut down and thrown into the fire. Thus you will know them by their fruits'.

The Acts 1 passage associates power received at Pentecost with being witnesses of Jesus Christ. How can you witness to Jesus Christ except by following in his footsteps and example? Jesus who self-emptied himself, associated with those on the margins of society, who denounced false religion which used tradition and a particular hermeneutic to justify excluding those it deemed unworthy, and who eventually was crucified in shame on a Roman cross as a common criminal, and yet does not respond in vengeance but in love, appealing for Peter to lay down his sword and to his father to forgive them 'for they know not what they do' (Luke 23:34). Instead, some have used this verse to justify craving after personal power (to give us wealth, health and success), rather than as a transformative power to challenge the structures of injustice and exclusion around us and to reach out to the outsider. But in the context when this verse was first articulated, the early church understood it in its true contextual meaning, for it was this verse which enabled them to be witnesses to Jesus Christ and his life, as they were empowered to boldly proclaim the coming of the kingdom of God, even as they were crucified, tortured and killed for their faith.

It is well known that Emperor Nero had Christians sewn-up in animal skins and throw them to the wild beasts to be devoured. He would also have them covered in pitch and use them as human torches to illumine his gardens. The verse in Acts 1 which tells of how the early Church were empowered to be followers of Christ, was about the power to stand up for one's beliefs in the face of persecution and torture, the power to not respond in violence to those who accuse you, and kill you and your family, the power of proclaiming a transformative love that had broken down the walls of exclusion between Jews and Gentiles. It was a power that had nothing to do with our modern day associations of power with wealth and political influence, for they had none. And similarly they did not articulate a theology of a powerful and interventionist God in terms of coming down from heaven and giving them military victory over their enemies (which had been a constant theme with their forebears from Joshua, King David, Samson etc), even though they believed God to be interventionist and powerful: but it was a radically new understanding of power and intervention, redefined by the cross. God had now intervened in human history, not by granting them a major military victory (as portrayed in the Old Testament narratives), but by showing a God who had taken on human flesh and loved to the end, dignifying the human condition and transforming the world through a love which reaches out and embraces all, even those who crucify him. This is a powerful 'event' (to reference Zizek again). But it is more than this. It is power redefined. Not the power of a political and militarised class, but power through weakness and shame, power manifested in vulnerability, power shown from the margins of acceptable society, and a power that ultimately breaks the power and grip of death, because love overcomes death. This is what we celebrate in the Eucharist. The 'givenness' of God. Christ who takes on human flesh for our salvation, and the salvation of the world. Christ who comes to show us what God is like. We often choose the path of our own selfish desires, our propensity for self-preservation at the expense of others, our ability to justify hatred and bitterness in our hearts towards those who hurt us....But Christ comes and shows us a better way. His incarnation into human history dignifies and redeems the human condition, reminding us that we are made in the very image of God. He calls us back to what is at the core of our being, which if we truly believed would mean that we could never dehumanise or scapegoat anyone else ever again, because they are made in the image of God, even if that image has been distorted and obfuscated by sin. Christ shows that the power of his undying love is transformative, and can change even the coldest of hearts who have been dehumanised by their own sin and shame. Those whose humanity has been deadened, are offered the possibility of being raised from the dead and into a life of dignity and worth, which when lived out in its fullness changes the world. It is a love that refuses to see the other as enemy, and is therefore fearless and able to face up to empire, torturers and accusers, and to respond in love and prayer, rather than violence and hatred. It is a kind of love that will not use the image of God as a tool to bring about the downfall of your enemies, but a love that subverts and transforms from within.

It is a picture of a God who is not up in the sky, pulling the strings of the world according to his will and holding on to some notion of omnipotence; but God Emmanuel down here. Suffering, loving, dying, resurrecting, reconciling with his creation, and thus transforming it through love. This is the good news, the evangel that we should proclaim with our lives. It is the culmination of the passage of the suffering servant in the Second Isaiah, recorded in chapter 53. And it is the hope of our world. This is the power exemplified by Christ, and the power given at Pentecost, which was to give the apostles and the early church the strength to die as martyrs in a political context where they were being dehumanised and scapegoated by the imperial regime. Christ's death on a Roman cross, identifies God with all those who have been scapegoated and dehumanised through human torture, and boldly proclaims that they are innocent. In identifying with those who are crushed by the systems of injustice and oppression, he dignifies their condition and offers the hope, as through his resurrection he defeats death and its power over us, and shows us that love with have the final word.

This redefinition of power is hardly the image of power that the pulpit-thumping prosperity gospel would associate with. The power proclaimed by preaching a gospel of prosperity is a very human understanding of power. The power preached from many other Christian denominations is not exempt from critique either, because it paints God into being a God who is powerful in a way that we imagine power to be exemplified: who at any moment could intervene in history and crush all our enemies and end all the world's wrongs with one strike of his hand. The longing for this kind of power goes back a long way and is deeply embedded in the human heart. It was that power which Satan tempted Christ with in the wilderness, where he promised him the kingdoms of this world. It was this view of power which Satan used to tempt Christ into throwing himself of a high point trusting that God would send angels to save him from falling to his death. It was this view of power that caused Peter to think that violence could be overcome with violence. And it is a power that is redefined at the cross, showing us that God's way is the way of love, even in the face of death., and that it is the through the power of this love that he is transforming the world from within, and calling us back to the core of our very being, as those who have been made in the image of God.

But this kind of power is seldom embodied by the church. In the charismatic circles which I was shaped in (and I value this tradition and see real worth in it) emphasises and took ownership of what was meant by the word 'healing'. The consequence was that healing became associated with individual healings (and there is a place and need for this, after all Christ was in the business of healing the sick); whereas the healing of society, injustice, war, and famine have all too often been neglected. This is not to say that there are many charismatics who have lived lives that served the poor and needy, and brought healing, restoration and love to those they have witnessed to (Jackie Pullinger, Bill Wilson and Heidi Baker are all cases in point). What I am getting at is a picture of God, which has for much of the 20th century put more emphasis on individual salvation and well-being above that of the welfare of humanity as a whole and the planet that sustains us. We are called not only to pray for the healing of the sick, but for the healing of our world. To heal the injustices of poverty and environmental degradation. To heal all that dehumanises and repays evil for evil. This is the way of Christ.

Both Judaism and Christianity place a high value on not only loving our neighbours and welcoming in the stranger, but also command us to love our enemies and to not repay evil with evil, but to do justice, seek reconciliation through sacrificial love. Unfortunately as history shows, the church has not always lived by these foundational truths, but has become too accommodating with power structures, it has lost its prophetic voice in terms of denouncing policies which promote and are complicit in systems of injustice. And because of this it has lost its moral authority. It is no coincidence that some of the most important social reformers of the past century led movements of non-violent resistance. Ghandi defeated an empire through subversive peaceful non-violent resistance. Martin Luther King changed a nation through his activism, church ministry, preaching and public speaking, Mother Teresa brought dignity and worth to the outcasts and those on the margins, and there are many more countless individuals who never made the news headlines engaged in the same transformational activity. These individuals had authority, which was much more transformative than power, which Tony Campolo spoke of in a session at the Greenbelt Festival in 2012.

The church has too often sought for power, and in doing so has lost its authority. The authority of Ghandi, Mother Teresa, Martin Luther King came from a living embodiment of the same self-sacrificial love that characterised Jesus' ministry on earth. That is, the full embodiment of a new way of living. Not seeking after material wealth, but seeking after justice, and association with those on the margins of society and the oppressed, a radical adherence to non-violence and love for all which enabled them to face their detractors without fear, and the willingness to lay down their lives for others.

If the church is going to have any place and relevance in our 21st world, it will be by rediscovering the core message of Christ which calls us to lay down our lives for the sake of others. This means that our worship and adoration of God is lived out in the pursuit of love of others. If we love others, then justice follows out as a direct result. It is impossible to love someone, and at the same time to enslave them. It is impossible to love them, and then kill them. To love is to do justice. If the church were to really do this, it would regain its authority. The tragedy is that throughout history it has sought power through earthly systems and methods, which do not bring true authority because they do not demand us to take up our cross. In fact earthy power operates in the exact opposite direction: through self-aggrandisement, through privilege, self-protection, upward mobility, earthly status, and often a craving for control. Christ calls us on a downward path of self-emptying. Resurrection and reconciling love comes not from a place of self-imposed power, but from laying our lives down in the service of others. It is this self-giving love which we celebrate at the Eucharist which we are called to embody.

Let us now look at how the craving for power has manifested itself throughout the history of the people of

God, from Old Testament times to our present day. This will be a whistle stop tour of but a few examples, as a full examination of this would run into many volumes.

One of the striking things about the Old Testament which can be traced throughout the canon is the way in which God relates to his people through punishment and blessing. Pick up any of the prophetic books and you will immediately see this cycle in action: the people of Israel sin, and God raises up other nations to punish them and takes them into exile. Vengeance and judgement is proclaimed by every Old Testament prophet to those who rebel against God, and I could begin to list verses to illustrate this, but they are so numerous and deeply embedded in our understanding of the God of the Old Testament (or as I would rather say, the depiction/understanding of God by the writers of the Old Testament), that I don't think that it is necessary.

God is depicted as a righteous judge, a jealous lover, and all-powerful deity who is a master of war and victorious in battle, and so on. We are well acquainted with these images. It was not just the Judaic tradition that depicted the God(s) of the universe in terms of judgement, but (amongst many others) the Babylonians, Sumerians and notably the Greeks. We have touched on elements of this in previous chapters, and will do so again. Many of the Greek gods sent punishments on their people. Hera, Zeus's wife and sister who came to be seen as the goddess of marriage (who, interestingly, was revered and worshiped as a virgin) would often vent her anger and punish her subjects, even if they had done nothing wrong. The Greek creation mythology (referenced briefly earlier in this book) presented the creation of the world as a violent struggle, where the various gods were in battle and competition with each other. Into the dark chaos, light and love emerge and the goddess Gaea (known as Mother Earth) and the god Ouranos (Father Sky) emerge and in turn create monsters with multiple heads who were powerful enough to raise mountains to the ground, and their strength was seen in the hurricane winds and volcanos. They also created the one eyed god Cyclopes, and the Titans (from where Zeus would come, as he was the son of the god of time Chronus). These monsters were banished to the underworld and chained up, but would later be released by god Zeus (interestingly who was endowed with the power of lightening and thunder) as he warred against his fellow gods (one of which was Atlas, who was condemned as a punishment to carry the world on his shoulder—which has interesting resonances with Christ who will bear the sins of the world on his shoulders).

What I am getting at is that we have to understand the Old Testament in the context in which it was written, when these myths proliferated and reflected the world views of the time. This does not detract from scripture, but rather opens it up. The idea of a Trinitarian Godhead, united in a relationship of mutual love (which of course would emerge much later, although is rooted in Old Testament scriptures as well as New) marks a radical shift away from the conflict which lies at the heart of how the gods are depicted in Greek mythology, warring and competing amongst themselves. The idea that will emerge so vividly in the New Testament of Father, Son and Holy Spirit in perfect union is unique and unprecedented in ancient world mythology.

Another point of differentiation which we observe throughout the Old Testament (which is why I mentioned the goddess Hera a few paragraphs ago) is that God never punishes people out of a whim: it is always because people sinned and departed from him. Hera would punish whenever she felt like it, and there was at times no reasoning behind it, and therefore no ethical framework to be learnt. In the Judaic scriptures, judgement and vengeance are always the consequence of wrongdoing. In the prophetic book of Amos for example, terrible judgement and punishment is proclaimed against the house of Israel. The reason given for this is for the way in which they had enriched themselves at the cost of the poor, and forgotten their own ancestral story as freed slaves from Egypt, set free and liberated by God. They had neglected the widow and the orphan, and had become complicit in the structures of greed and privilege, whilst neglecting the vulnerable. And God is depicted as full of wrath and anger, in a language and imagery which often appears shocking to us in our day an age. But we need to consider when this was written, and consider what is going on here, for this is a very different image of a god to that of Hera. And it is the process of differentiation that really interests me here, because by portraying God in the Old Testament as a deity who punishes evil and rewards good, lays the basis for an ethical framework of human accountability. It teaches us that our actions have profound consequences for our fellow human beings. It denounces greed, selfishness and a rejection of the divine as punishable; because when we forget that we our fellow human beings are made in the image of God, it becomes much easier to dehumanise them. All torture, genocide and pogroms can only be inflicted once the victims have been dehumanised. We must remember that the ancestral children of Israel, such as Joshua were not exempt from the sin of dehumanising the other, and of course justified their genocidal actions by claiming that it was mandated by God.

What is strikingly different in the Judaic tradition (and just as much as judgement, wrath and anger feature in the

Old Testament prophetic books, so does mercy, love and restoration) is that judgement does not have the final word. There is always the promise of restoration, reconciliation and shalom. Yes, God is depicted as wrathful and vengeful; there is no question about this, and it must be faced head on. But he is also depicted as forgiving, liberating and a God of restoration and reconciliation, and often relenting from his anger and driven to compassion.

This is how the scriptures portray God, and in this paradigm we can learn essential truths about the human condition, about our responsibilities as human beings living in the fragile community of our world, threatened by the same sins denounced in the times of the prophets. Greed, lust for power and wealth, a neglect of the poor and the vulnerable, and a rejection of the divine, can lead to us to dehumanising the other and forgetting that they are endowed with dignity, because they are made in God's image.

That is why, when religion is used to justify the lust for power, position, wealth, and the neglect of the poor and the marginalised, then it is a religion under judgement, and as the poet Bernard Shaw said (in the context of World War I and the Russian Revolution) that 'God's wrath is heavy on us'.

Many have pointed to the conversion of Roman Emperor Constantine for a major change which occurs with how Christianity evolves. As we know, Constantine converted to Christianity, and made it the official religion of state, and in 313 issued an edict decriminalising Christianity. The progressive shift of the Roman Empire from endorsing and promoting a view of pagan religion comprised of many gods, to Christian monotheism, profoundly shapes the evolution of Christianity. I have heard Father Richard Rohr say on several occasions (and I paraphrase from memory so these words are not the exact words, but capture the point I want to make) saying that when you transition from being a religion lived out on the margins of empire, being persecuted in the catacombs, to become the religion of empire, where you are the army, the state and so on, it affects the way you see yourself, and the way in which you read scripture.

There is no question that a monotheistic belief system allows you to unite disparate and at times conflicting religious views, and galvanise a divided people under one common cause.

This is what happened in the history of Spain. In 1475 the kingdoms of Aragon and Castile were brought together by the political marriage of Ferdinand of Aragon and Isabel of Castile. Their union united the divided kingdoms of Spain, was blessed by the Pope, and they imposed their version of Catholic faith on a divided nation to unify it. The ongoing struggle against the Muslims in Spain (known as the *Renconquista* and which had existed in some form during the 800 years the Moors were a powerful presence in Spain) culminated during the reign of Isabel and Ferdinand (also known as The Catholic Kings), and Spain rose to become one of the world's greatest empires. King Phillip the II would later boast that the sun never set on the Spanish empire, given their expansive conquest and appropriation of foreign territories.

Their plunder of gold and silver, natural and human resources throughout Latin America and beyond, enforced through an unholy union of church and crown which imposed its narrow views through the state sponsored torture device of the Inquisition, is well known, and therefore will not be explored in any depth here. Suffice to say that the Spanish Empire of the 16th and 17th centuries constitutes a good example of how religion and state can conspire in the business of exploitation, theft and torture, and the use of religion as a galvanising and justifying force to masquerade the exploitation, torture and greed. Many of you will have seen Roland Joffe's film *The Mission*, which portrays both Spanish and Portuguese settler violence.

Of course, you don't need religion to do this, as the 20th century shows. Mao, Stalin, the Khmer Rouge and Hitler caused the death and suffering of millions, by using intractable political systems that inculcated dehumanisation and death (be it through National Socialism/Fascism or Communism). The history of humanity shows that violence and the lust for power lie deeply embedded in the human condition, and if this goes unchecked, will use whatever at its disposal (be it religion or non-religious systems of control) for its own ends. I will not labour this point as I am reliably confident that it will be obvious to most readers, and as this book is about religion, both its possibilities and abuses, I am deliberately critiquing the unholy alliance between the pursuit of power and control and religion, and take for granted that more violence has been carried out in the name of other death-driven ideologies than in the name of religion (although current day Islamist terrorism has become one of the major threats to civilisation in the 21st century), together with wealth inequality and the global arms race.

Sticking with the example of Spain for a moment or two (I know Spain well as I lived there as a child, studied Spanish literature at university and taught in the Hispanic studies department of Glasgow University before training for ministry), it is a good example of how badly wrong it can go when religion and power are linked hand in hand, in a context of extreme ideological views. During the Spanish Civil War (1936-1939) much of the Catholic Church and ecclesial establishment supported Franco's coalition of the extreme Right. When Franco won the war in 1939, the Church was handed control of the Spanish education system, and enjoyed a prominent role in the repressive dictatorship that followed. The damage this has done to the church's reputation in Spain has not been healed. It is important to understand that the forces of the political left in Spain are to blame as well for this: throughout the early 20th century it actively encouraged anticlericalism, which often resulted in the burning of churches and desecration of sacred spaces. Many nuns and priests were killed. And during Spain's brief and fragile experiment with democracy (1931-1936), the centre left coalition of Republicans (in power between 1931-1933) did nothing to stop the violence directed at the church. At one level, it is understandable why the church would see its survival only possible with Franco's Nationalists, as it could not expect any favours from the other side. This, does not justify the church's complicity in propping up a dictatorship that used torture and severe repression (especially in the early years following the Civil War), and is a good example of what happens when the church (through fear) loses its prophetic voice and seeks protection from the political establishment. There was no 'confessing church' in Spain as there was in Germany, when Theologian Dietrich Bonhoeffer denounced the Third Reich and broke away from the mainstream church which was complicit with the consolidation of fascism. We all know this aspect of history well, so I won't expand on it. I am just referencing it briefly as it is a good example of what can happen when the church is too accommodating with political power, and overly obsessed with its own preservation and survival.

Even today in 21st century Spain, there persists a strong anti-clericalism, and much of the intelligentsia on the left adopt ardent humanist positions which are anti-church. I was on the streets in Madrid during the severe economic recession following the 2008 world economic collapse, and amongst the thousands of youth who were protesting against austerity and camping out in the centre of Madrid, there was a strong anticlerical sentiment. There was no presence of the church, even though many food banks, soup kitchens and charitable work is carried out by the church. Spain is still polarised, locked in a dualistic battle between Left and Right, where progressive thinking is deemed to be on the Left where the church is not welcome. When you contrast this with Britain, where church leaders and progressive thinkers from across the political divide will converge on anti-poverty marches, it is a far cry from the situation in Spain, which politically is still at a fairly infantile and reactionary stage, given that democracy is still a relatively recent phenomenon.

What this illustrates are the dangers for the church when it aligns itself too closely with power. It also highlights the tunnel-vision of much of the political left in Spain, who position themselves as anti-church. There needs to be a far more mature engagement between progressive thinking by those within and outside of the church (as there is in the UK) as issues of poverty, injustice, and the plight of thousands of migrants risking their lives on make-shift rafts to reach Spain; are current issues which would unite the church and its detractors in radical social action, rather than fuelling ongoing suspicion and antagonism.

Of course, Spain is only one example of what can happen when, in a divided society, the church (historically) is seen to be on one side and not the other. All the good work that the Spanish Catholic church has done in terms of poverty relief, community building and helping those on the margins of society must not be forgotten. The polarisation in Spain between a progressive left who largely want nothing to do with religion and a

State Church that has been seen as an impediment to social change, has not served the people of Spain well. It would be far more healthy for the voices from within the Spanish Catholic Church who want to bring about a more just society to join with voices from across the social-political spectrum and work the common good, despite any ideological differences.

The challenge for the church, not only in Spain but across the western world where it is in such decline, is to become the church of social justice. Until the Church regains is prophetic voice to denounce the structures of injustice, and offers an alternative liturgical rhythm to the pounding drum of excessive consumerism and wealth accumulation in the western world, then it will continue to decline and disappear down the slow path of irrelevance and oblivion. It will become little more than a private members club, ticking along nicely within the prevailing structures of the day, challenging nothing, but just managing decline. The church can provide a space for spiritual renewal and transformation, and embody a narrative where all are welcome, and where no one is excluded because of background, politics, or gender.

Chapter 5

Broken God

God as a Highest Being—a steady hand at the wheel of the universe, ordering all things to good purpose, the spanning providential eye o' seeing all—has had a good run. (John Caputo)[49]

But he said unto me, 'My grace is sufficient for you, for power is made perfect in weakness. So I will boast all the more gladly of my weaknesses, so that the power of Christ may dwell in me'. (2 Corinthians 12:9)

I am wounded by theology, unhinged and uprooted by the blow it has delivered to my heart. (John Caputo)[50]

In the previous chapter we examined the pitfalls of the Christian religion when it becomes too intoxicated with power and the pursuit of individual wealth. In this chapter I want to think about the idea of a God who is not revealed and manifested in power-play, but in weakness. This view of God is of course nothing new, and for those of you interested in pursuing this further, you should read the works of John Caputo and process theologians such as

---

[49] John Caputo, *The Insistence of God: A Theology of Perhaps* (Bloomington &Indianapolis: Indiana U.P.,Indiana Series in the Philosophy of Religion, 2013) [loc 60-61, Kindle Edition].
[50] John Caputo, *The Weakness of God: A Theology of the Event* (Bloomington & Indianapolis: Indiana U.P.,Indiana Series in the Philosophy of Religion, 2006), 1.

Catherine Keller, John Cobb Jr and Charles Hartshorne.[51] I will be drawing on their ideas in this chapter.

Of course, it was the apostle Paul (following in the traditions of Old Testament literature such as the suffering servant as written about by the Second Isaiah) who foregrounded weakness as the way in which God's power is shown. In 2 Corinthians 12:9 it reads 'My grace is sufficient for you, for power is made perfect in weakness. So I will boast all the more gladly of my weaknesses, so that the power of Christ may dwell in me'. Written at a time when the dominating world power was Rome, and the Jews had been expecting a Messiah who would win a military victory over Rome, Corinthians 12:9 is nothing short of revolutionary. It marks a paradigm shifting moment in Scripture; a real epiphany of what God is like, and it shows how Paul was gifted with incredible revelatory insights into the nature of God. Pause and think about the context in which this verse was written. We know that Paul's books were written before the gospels, and very close to the event of the crucifixion, and that Paul was put to death before the fall of Jerusalem in AD 70. This makes what Paul is saying even more striking: an event which had caused many of Jesus' followers to abandon him, and in the case of Peter, deny him; an event which was seen as shameful defeat to the Roman Empire, is depicted here as actually revealing a God whose influence and power is brought about through weakness (although in that 'weakness' there was real strength). The Messiah not only bears the shame of not being a military leader who could free the Jewish

---

[51] Although the name of John Caputo appears alongside well-known Process Theologians here, it is important to emphasise that Caputo is not a Process theologian. Caputo has no interest in Process theology, which he sees as falling into the trap of metaphysics. But the critique of an all-powerful God is something that both Caputo and Process theologians share, although from a different philosophical angle.

people from occupation, but undergoes the indignity of dying a death reserved for criminals and outcasts. God's identification with frail humanity and the outsider is complete, and the love, solidarity, and reconciliation of such an event leaves its indelible mark on human history, dividing it into a before and after.

Paul was one of the first to understand this, and it is little wonder that Harold Bloom includes him in his pantheon of 'geniuses', stating that:

It is easy for many Americans to mistake Paul as a revivalist, whose total emphasis is upon rebirth through the forgiveness of sin. That is a weak misreading of Paul, who was more than an apostle of grace. The former Pharisee was a great inventor who transformed Hellenistic Christianity into a new kind of world religion.[52]

Paul sets Jesus within the Judaic traditions, as the culmination of the Law. As Bloom (and others) have argued, Paul is not so interested in depicting the 'historical Jesus', but Christ, as revelation of what God is like. Through the death on the cross, Jesus Christ becomes representative of a new divine economy in Paul's mind, which liberates the world through apparent weakness and folly, as set out in his first letter to the Corinthians:

For the message about the cross is foolishness to those who are perishing, but to us who are being saved it is the power of God. For it is written: 'I will destroy the wisdom of the wise, and the discernment of the discerning I will thwart'. Where is the one who is wise? Where is the scribe? Where is the debater of this age? Has not God made foolish the wisdom of the world? For since, in the wisdom of God, the world did not know God through wisdom, God decides through the foolishness of our proclamation, to save those who believe. For Jews demand signs

---

[52] Harold Bloom, *Genius: A Mosaic of One Hundred Exemplary Creative Minds* (London: Fourth Estate, 2002), 142.

and Greek's desire wisdom, but we proclaim Christ crucified, a stumbling-block to Jews and foolishness to Gentiles, but to those who are called, both Jews and Greeks, Christ the power of God and the wisdom of God.
Broken God

For God's foolishness is wiser than human wisdom, and God's weakness is stronger than human strength. (1 Corinthians 1: 18-25)

Worldly definitions of power and wisdom are subverted. The infamy, shame and 'weakness' of Jesus' death on the cross, is now understood as the way in which not only identifies with those crushed by military empire and executed outside the walls of the city, to leave in no doubt, their expulsion from imperial society as exiles. It associates God with the outsider, with the one who is calumniated, weak, in the eyes of religious and military power, and turns the 'foolishness' and 'weakness' of the event, into a moment of salvitic power. It represents the breaking down between barriers, as is central in Paul's text cited above, as Jews and Greeks are welcomed, echoing Paul's earlier world-changing verse which sets Jews and Gentiles, men and women, slaves and free; as one:

There is no longer Jew or Greek, there is no longer slave or free, there is no longer male and female, for all of you are one in Christ Jesus. And if you belong to Christ, then you are Abraham's offspring, heirs according to promise. (Galatians 3:28-29)

The transition is now complete: the call of Christ is open to all, and there is to be no differentiation or discrimination based on ethnicity, economic status or gender, for we all come as equals to Christ. We all come recognising our need for salvation, from ourselves, from our sin, from our deep rooted propensity to put our needs and wants above those of others.

God's fullest revelation has come in Christ. And the means by which he brings about salvation and hope, could not be more counter-intuitive to what the Jews were expecting. Throughout their troubled history, of enslavement and exile, the children of Israel had had to contend with the big imperial powers of the day: Egypt, Assyria, Babylon and Rome. It was understandable that they were expecting a military leader who would free them from oppression through military might, after all, throughout the Old Testament Yahweh is depicted as the warrior-God, raising up leaders such as Moses, Joshua and King David who would kill in the name of God.

But Christ's power is manifested in a radically different way. His struggle is a different one. The name Jesus is a derivative of Joshua no less, subverts military and earthly might from within. If Joshua was one of the most celebrated military leaders in Jewish history, leading the children of Israel into the promised land; Jesus (the new Joshua), radically subverts the very roots of his own name, refusing to meet violence with violence, but liberating and bringing hope through non-violent resistance and out-poured love. A love that is not contained or directed simply at his followers, but which breaks down all national, social, economic, religious and gender barriers, as the apostle Paul understood.

Jesus fights a different fight. Not the way Joshua did, by crushing his enemies though military might, not the way Elijah did by calling down fire on his enemies, not the way King David did who gloried in the number of his victims, but one whose mission is one of restoring dignity to the outcast. His mission brings liberation and a rearranging of society by challenging the structures of injustice and exclusion, perpetrated by the military imperial rule and the religious authorities.

It takes great courage to adopt a position of non-violence, as Christ's example shows. Our natural instinct is to protect ourselves through force, but Jesus refuses that path, when he tells Peter to put away his sword: 'Put your sword back into its place; for all who take the sword will perish by the sword. Do you not think that I cannot appeal to my Father, and he will at once send me more than twelve legions of angels?' (Matthew 26: 52-53). In Luke's account, we see Jesus touching and healing the ear of the servant of the high priest, showing the healing that comes through non-violence:

When those who were around him saw what was coming, they asked, 'Lord, should we strike with the sword?' Then one of them struck the slave of the high priest and cut off his right ear. But Jesus said 'No more of this!' And he touched his ear and healed him. (Luke 22: 49-51)

This dramatic scene leading up to the crucifixion boldly shows the restorative and healing nature of non-violent resistance. It shows that healing and restoration follow non-violent resistance.

As I write this, coalition forces are pulling out their troops from a 13 year war in Afghanistan. The purpose of the war was to root-out the Taliban following the attacks of 9/11 on American soil. The Taliban, as we know, had imposed sharia law, banning women from education, prohibiting them from working unless it was in the home, public floggings if they did not adhere to Islamic dress codes, public stoning of women accused or suspected of adultery, banned music, films, killing anyone who converts from Islam to another religion, and the list goes on.

After 13 years of war, and casualties of both civilians and coalition forces running into thousands, and in addition to the human cost, an estimated cost (to the American tax payer, not counting that of the other coalition partners) of approximately $1 trillion. That is $1,000,000,000,000 (one million million). Over 13 years, that roughly equates to $210,748,155.954 a day, or $8,781,173.164 per hour or if you break it down by the minute, about $146,352.886 for every minute of war.

The human and economic costs of Afghanistan were huge (although relatively small in comparison with the War in Iraq from, where it is estimated that around half a million lost their lives, at a cost to the USA of over $2 trillion—just double the numbers given above). But these are conservative estimates. On the 29th of March 2013, *The Daily Telegraph* (hardly a left-leaning anti-war paper) reported that the combined cost of the Iraq and Afghan wars was nearer $6 trillion.[53]

Simply detailing the military costs of the major partners in the wars, does not do justice to the thousands of human casualties, in addition to those injured and invalidated for life. Then there are the damage done to infrastructure, ancient historic civilisations, and the ecological devastation.

But the other issue patently obvious here, is that both these wars have not worked. The Taliban are back in Afghanistan, and Iraq has descended into a full blown sectarian civil war between Sunni and Shia, with Isis now thrown into the mix. I wonder what would have been the result if the same amounts of money had been spent on social justice, on peace and reconciliation initiatives, on eliminating many of the grievances which make young men especially vulnerable to radicalisation.

---

[53] Peter Foster, 'Cost to US of Iraq and Afghan Wars could hit $6 trillion', *The Telegraph*, (29.3.2013).
[http://www.telegraph.co.uk/news/worldnews/northamerica/USA/9961877/Cost-to-US-of -Iraq-and-Afghan-wars-could-hit-6-trillion.html], accessed on (30.1.2015).

On the 9th of October, 2012, schoolgirl Malala Yousafzai was shot in the head by a Taliban gunman, whilst she travelled to school, in the Swat Valley of northwest Pakistan (many of the Taliban forces had retreated and regrouped here following the coalition invasion of Afghanistan). Malala had been boldly promoting education for girls and bravely writing about life as a young girl under Taliban rule. She was fortunate to survive, and spent some time in the Queen Elizabeth Hospital in Birmingham (U.K.) where she received specialist treatment. In 2013 she appeared on the front cover the *Time* magazine, recognised as one of the most 100 influential people in the world, and in 2014 was co-awarded the Nobel Peace Prize.

My question is: what was more effective in terms of drawing attention to the plight of girls under the Taliban and standing up to its terror from within? $8,781,173.164 spent every hour over 13 years of war by the USA alone (in addition to the human cost)? Or the bold defiance and courage of a young Pakistani girl? What would have inspired thousands of Muslim girls across the globe about the value of education and their right to it, and showed up the Taliban for what it was? How many lives and expense could have been saved by funding local educational initiatives, and addressing social inequality, which is not an excuse for or explanation of terrorism, but is undoubtedly a breeding ground for young recruits who have little sense of purpose or prospects? What does Malala teach us about power, weakness, military strength and non-violent resistance?

Earlier in this chapter we referenced the words of father John Dear, the Jesuit peace activist who, through his life and writings, has done more than most to promote the cause of non-violent resistance. In the following quotation, he cites the words of Gandhi, reminding us of the power of non-violence:

Humanity has to get out of violence only through nonviolence', Ghandi declared. 'Hatred can only be overcome by love. Counter-hatred only increases the surface so well as the depth of hatred'. 'Nonviolence is the greatest and most active force in the world. One person who can express nonviolence in life exercises a force superior to all the forces of brutality'. 'The force generated by nonviolence is infinitely greater than the force of all the arms invented by humanity's ingenuity.[54]

A few pages on, John Dear strips away perceptions of God as violent, to remind us of how Christ reveals who God really is like, subverting and questioning the way in which God was depicted and understood in certain passages of the Old Testament:

The God of Jesus is a God of nonviolence. The cross demonstrates to us that God suffers human violence without retaliating and transforms us with forgiving love [...] Yet how far we have come from this image of the nonviolent God! Most Christians today imagine God as wrathful, vengeful, angry, bitter, mean, unjust, terrifying and violent, even though their personal experience of God may be as a living presence of love [...] God calls all of us to resist the forces of death, but only to do so with God's own active love. God invites us, primarily through the life of Jesus, to participate in God's own nonviolence. God does not sit idly by and allow the violence of the world to continue. God resists violence but does not use violence to resist. God's love is transforming the world's violence.

God does not and cannot use violence to change the world. Though ancient scriptures and texts portray God as violent, the life of Jesus reveals that God is nonviolent. Jesus teaches us that. God does not use violence; rather, God uses active love and truth to resolve conflict and save humanity. For many, then, God is not all-powerful, as Aquinas writes long ago that is, if power is understood as violent force. Instead, God is powerless. Like the poor of the earth, God is the power of nonviolence, the 'powerless power' that refrains from violence but insists on truth and justice

---

[54] John Dear, *The God of Peace*, 11.

through love. God does not uses the 'power' of violence to change our hearts, to end warm to end systemic injustice and world poverty. Instead, God sides with the poor, touches our hearts, and invites us to become God's instruments of active nonviolence to transform the world into God's reign of justice and peace. Such an image of God invites our ongoing conversation toward a deeper, more active nonviolence.[55]

John Dear taps into one of the deep mysteries of God, hinted at by Apostle Paul when he writes about 'power made perfect in weakness'. God is not a coercive force, but as it says in 1 John 4:7, God is love: 'Beloved, let us love one another, because love is from God; everyone who loves is born of God and knows God. Whoever does not love does not know God, for God is love'.

Traditional Christianity has been struggling through the centuries, attempting to defend God in the face of so much suffering in our world. If God is all powerful, why did He not intervene to stop Auschwitz, the genocide in Rwanda, the abduction of the schoolgirls by Boko Haram in Northern Nigeria, the deaths of thousands of children dying from starvation, the persecution and torture of Christians in Northern Iraq, Pakistan, North Korea and many other countries?

If he is all knowing and outside of space and time and therefore knows the future, why set the whole world in motion in the first place, if it was to bring about so much heart-wrenching suffering? How can God be all powerful and omniscient and good at the same time?

As I write this, social media is awash with criticism of religion and God. British actor and writer Stephen Fry

---

[55]John Dear, *The God of Peace*, 30-32.

suggested that if God does exist, then he must be an 'evil, capricious monstrous maniac'.[56] Many of my Christian friends have posted elaborate challenges to Fry, engaging in 'Facebook theodicy', trying to vindicate and justify God. Attempting to argue (as I did for many years) that God is all powerful and all loving, but will not intervene to stop the evils in the world because he has given us free choice, no longer convinces me as a line of argument. I used to believe this, although it always left me unsatisfied as an explanation, and it would be very difficult to say this to an African mother who has held her dying baby in her arms, unable to feed it. But I don't believe this about God anymore. Before I go on to outline a different view of God, here is an extract of the article in *The Guardian* which caused so much polemic in the Christian community:

In his imaginary conversation with God, Fry says he would tell him: 'How dare you create a world in which there is such misery that is not our fault? It's not right'.

'It's utterly, utterly evil. Why should I respect a capricious, mean-minded, stupid God who creates a world which is so full of injustice and pain?'

Pressed by Byrne over how he would react if he was locked outside the pearly gates, Fry says: 'I would say: 'bone cancer in children? What's that about?'

'Because the God who created this universe, if it was created by God, is quite clearly a maniac, utter maniac. Totally selfish. We

---

[56] Henry MacDonald, 'Stephen Fry Calls God 'An Evil, Capricious, Monstrous, Maniac', (1st of February 2015) [http://www.theguardian.com/culture/2015/feb/01/stephen-fry-god-evil-maniac-irish-tv http://www.theguardian.com/culture/2015/feb/01/stephen-fry-god-evil-maniac-irish-tv], accessed 5.2.2015.

have to spend our life on our knees thanking him?! What kind of god would do that?'

On how to explain the wonders of the world, Fry then launches an another attack on all seeing, all knowing God creator.

'Yes, the world is very splendid but it also has in it insects whose whole lifecycle is to burrow into the eyes of children and make them blind. They eat outwards from the eyes. Why? Why did you do that to us? You could easily have made a creation in which that didn't exist. It is simply not acceptable.

'It's perfectly apparent that he is monstrous. Utterly monstrous and deserves no respect whatsoever. The moment you banish him, life becomes simpler, purer, cleaner, more worth living in my opinion.'[57]

I would suggest that if God is all powerful, all knowing, and had had the option of creating the world in a different way, then Stephen Fry has a point.

For life we need ecosystems, and ecosystems rely on predation, food chains, suffering, as we considered in chapter one. There is no conceivable way we could have our world without ecosystems, it would be like Mars or the Moon: there would be no life, which is why the fanciful idea which emerges from a literal belief in The Garden of Eden, where everything is 'perfect' but then changes after the disobedience of Adam and Eve, makes no plausible sense.

---

[57] Henry MacDonald, 'Stephen Fry Calls God 'An Evil, Capricious, Monstrous, Maniac', (1st of February 2015)
[http://www.theguardian.com/culture/2015/feb/01/stephen-fry-god-evil-maniac-irish-tv
http://www.theguardian.com/culture/2015/feb/01/stephen-fry-god-evil-maniac-irish-tv], accessed 5.2.2015.

Broken God

But I do not believe in a God who is all powerful and all knowing. I used to, but that image of God died in Auschwitz, in Rwanda, in the killing fields of Vietnam, in the 2004 Tsunami, and so many other countless human and natural tragedies through the ages of human history.

Elie Wiesel, the survivor from Auschwitz, where he witnessed the death of his parents, sister, and thousands of his fellow Jews (in addition to gypsies and Polish 'rebels') wrote in his memoir *Night*:

Never shall I forget that night, the first night in camp, that turned my life into one long night seven times sealed.
Never shall I forget that smoke.
Never shall I forget the small faces of the children whose bodies I saw transformed into smoke under a silent sky.
Never shall I forget those flames that consumed my faith forever.
Never shall I forget the nocturnal silence that deprived me for all eternity of the desire to live.
Never shall I forget those moments that murdered my God and my soul and turned my dreams to ashes.
Never shall I forget these things, even were I condemned to live as long as God Himself.
Never.[58]

The Holocaust brings about a renewed questioning about the existence of God. We know from history that it was not the only time the Jewish people had suffered terrible inhumanity and dehumanisation at the hands of those who saw them as a threat, but there is something terrifying and deeply traumatic to see how such genocide and extermination can happen in one of the most culturally developed nations of the West at the height of modernity in the 20th century.

---

[58] Elie Wiesel, *Night,* translated from French by Marion Wiesel (London: Penguin Books, 2006), xix.

This is not the place to begin reflecting on the reasons why it happened, as there are countless books and articles on the subject already. What the remainder of this chapter will focus on is the extent to which belief in an all-powerful, omniscient God is possible after Auschwitz. Auschwitz stretches orthodox theodicy to breaking point: if God is all good, and all powerful, how can stand by and witness the atrocities of Auschwitz?

There is a strand of theology which takes a radical departure from the orthodox view of God as all powerful. It argues that God is not all powerful, but all loving. God is not seated on the throne of heaven, watching the events on earth descend into cruel suffering and chaos, deciding to intervene here but not there, able to bring suffering to an end but choosing not; but God is down here, suffering with those who suffer, and opening up the possibilities of love and compassion within a world bent of dehumanising cruelty. It is important to note that even those who hold to an orthodox view of God as all powerful would agree with us thus far, the crucial difference is that orthodoxy purports that God in his infinite wisdom, and because he has gifted us with free will, will not intervene to stop evil every time a human being commits an act of terror, because that would eliminate free choice, and turn humankind into some sort of automaton. I have some sympathy with this view, and for much of my life I have defended it, but it has always left me unsatisfied in the face of horrific suffering, and with the underlying question as to why God does not bring it all to an end.

Caputo's theology takes a different view, and drawing on the writings of Paul, believes that God's 'power' is not to be understood in terms of human power, but as 'power made perfect in weakness'. The cross undergoes a radical reinterpretation: Jesus's sacrifice on the cross is not to satisfy an all-powerful God up in the sky, who gets so angry about sin that the only way He can bring himself to forgive humanity is by demanding that an innocent victim be brutally tortured (which in effect would make God no better that the countless mythical Gods down the century who demanded blood sacrifice to appease their anger); but God is the innocent victim, immolated and tortured by a world which has rejected the way of love. By loving in the face of hatred, and pronouncing blessing on those whose persecute him, and refusing to retaliate by using violence, Christ opens up the possibility of a new way of living. The weakness of the cross is transformed into a moment of power, but not power as understood as coercive, but the incarnate power of suffering love, which loves to the end.

We have already explored aspects of this in an earlier chapter of this book, so I will not rehearse the same arguments now. Caputo's theology strips away both the comfort and the discomfort of belief in an all-powerful God. That God has died. Instead, God is understood as a 'weak' force, bringing the possibility of love and reconciliation out of hate, just as he brought order out of 'watery chaos' (to use a phrase from Catherine Keller) in Genesis 1.

Philosopher and theologian John Caputo is one of the key thinkers and practitioners of the idea of God as not all powerful. In his book *The Weakness of God: A Theology of the Event*, he tries to get us to differentiate between the name of 'God', and what that name harbours. Drawing on the work of philosopher Jacques Derrida and the writings of the apostle Paul, he deconstructs our preconceived notions of an all-powerful God, and leaves us holding on to faith by our finger tips, as the whole edifice and security of orthodox belief comes crashing down. But this does not mark the end of faith, or the end of God. Rather, it opens up new possibilities, where faith is tested to breaking point, where faith coexists with doubt, and where faith no longer brings the comfort of believing in the strong edifice of belief which we have built up over the centuries. But it is a faith that dares to believe in the possibility of reconstruction from amongst the rubble. There is a sense in which more faith is needed when this happens, not less.

For much of my Christian life, I have believed the foundational axioms of orthodox faith: God is the all-powerful creator God, who creates out of nothing, who controls the events of history and who one day will punish unbelievers in the eternal fires of hell whilst those fortunate enough to have been converted to Christianity will enjoy eternity in heaven. Evil happens because of human fallenness, and God intervenes at the crucifixion to punish evil by pouring out his wrath (which he takes upon himself). He could intervene and stop the course of history and evil in its tracks, but chooses not to because he has given humankind free will, and if he were to intervene every time an act of evil happened, then there would be no freedom to speak of. But there will be a day when this world we be brought to an end (although the eternal fires of hell await those who have rejected God, or believed in a different God).

This is broad-brush, but captures the essentials of this kind of faith. We get round the theodicy difficulties by appealing to the idea that all will be well in the end (at least for us Christians) and by appealing to the freedom of will argument.

Caputo's theology (and much of Process Theology for that matter) offers no such comfort/discomfort (depending on your view). The God described above has died. Died in the pogroms. Died in the torture chambers where the blood of the innocent cries out down the centuries. Died in the gas chambers of the torture chambers and death camps. Elie Wiesel recounts the following horrific event, which he recalls from his time in Auschwitz, which I will quote in full:

The SS seemed more preoccupied, more worried, than usual. To hand a child in front of thousands of onlookers was not a small matter. The head of the camp read the verdict. All eyes were on the child. He was pale, almost calm, but he was biting his lips as he stood in the shadows of the gallows.

This time, the *Lagerkapo* refused to act as executioner. Three SS took his place.

The three condemned prisoners together stepped onto the chairs. In unison, the nooses were placed around their necks.

'Long live liberty!', shouted the two men.

But the boy was silent.

'Where is merciful God, where is He? Someone behind me was asking.

At the signal, the three chairs were tipped over.

Total silence in the camp. On the horizon, the sun was setting.

'Caps off'! Screamed the *Laheralteste*. His voice quivered. As for the rest of us we we weeping.

'Cover your heads' !

Then came the March past the victims. The two men were no longer alive. Their tongues were hanging out, swollen and bluish.

But the third rope was still moving: the child, too light, was still breathing...

And so he remained for more than half an hour, lingering between life and death, writhing before our eyes. And we were forced to look at him at close range.

He was still alive when I passed him. Hs tongue was still red, his eyes not yet extinguished.

Behind me, I heard the same man asking:

'For God's sake, where is God'?

And from within me, I heard a voice answer:

'Where He is? This is where--hanging here from this gallows...'

That night, the soup tasted of corpses.[59]

---

[59] Elie Wiesel, *Night*. Translated from the French by Marion Wiesel (London: Penguin Books, 2006), 64-65.

In the Forward to this edition of *Night* Francois Mauriac recounts on how Elie Wiesel, who was still a child when he lost his mother, sister, and other members of his family who were gassed to death in Auschwitz, and also witnessed the barbaric cruelty and inhumanity of the hangings, referenced above, comments on the effect all of this had on Elie Wiesel:

On the last day of the Jewish year, the child is present at the Solomon ceremony of Rosh Hashanah. He hears thousands of slaves cry out in unison, 'Blessed be the Almighty'! Not so long ago he too would have knelt down, and with such worship, such awe, such love! But this day, he does not kneel, he stands. The human creature, humiliated and offended in ways that are inconceivable to the mind or the heart, defies the blind and deaf divinity.

And this is how Elie Wiesel recounts in his own words how he felt:

I no longer pleaded for anything. I was no longer able to lament. On the contrary, I felt very strong. I was the accuser, God the accused. My eyes had opened and I was alone, terribly alone in a world without God, without man. Without love or mercy. I was nothing but ashes now, but I felt myself to be stronger than this Almighty to whom my life had been bound for so long. In the midst of these men assembled for prayer, I felt like an observer, a stranger.[60]

Human suffering on this scale almost always causes us to question our faith and belief in God. And so it should...Our questioning articulates that something is profoundly wrong with the world. It struggles with the absurdity of belief in an all-powerful being who could at any moment step in a put an end to it, and yet chooses not to. In Albert Camus' novel *The Plague*, some of the

---

[60] Wiesel, *Night*, xx.

characters voice the sense of living in a world where God is either dead or has withdrawn from the world:

'After all...', the doctor continued, hesitating again and looking closely at Tarrou. 'And this is something that a man like you might understand; since the order of the world is governed by death, perhaps it is better for God that we should not believe in Him and struggle with all our strength against death, without raising our eyes to heaven and to His silence'.[61]

It is understandable that existentialism as a philosophical and literary movement was consolidated in the years between World War I and World War II, although had its seeds in writers and thinkers such as Kierkegaard, Nietzsche, Unamuno, Schopenhauer and Kafka. If all religion can offer you is the picture of an all-powerful God, able to put an end to suffering but choosing not to, creating the world only then to withdraw as it races towards self-destruction, then it is understandable that many rejected religion all together.

The existentialism of Albert Camus and Jean Paul Sartre sees humankind as all alone, in an absurd universe into which they have been born without any choice, and yet, with the burden of responsibility for their actions. The onus is on the individual to accept this, and to face the consequences of his or her actions.

Franz Kafka captured the existential plight of the human condition in his novel *The Trial* (1925), which narrates how office worker Joseph K is arrested one morning in his home, for reasons he is never told of. The novel charts Joseph K's attempt to prove his innocence to the faceless judges and authorities, but does not succeed in doing so, and is executed at end of the novel.

---

[61] Albert Camus, *The Plague.* Translated by Robin Buss with an introduction by Tony Judt (London: Penguin Books, 2001), 98.

Throughout the novel there is a strong sense that Joseph K faces his dilemma alone. There are other characters in the book who offer him some assistance and companionship, but ultimately, his doomed quest for justice is something he must face alone. *The Trial* develops themes already set out in one of Kafka's short stories *Before the Law*, about a man who waits all his life to be admitted to the law:

> Before he dies, all his experiences in these long years gather themselves in his head to one point, a question he has not yet asked the doorkeeper. He waves him nearer, since he can no longer raise his stiffening body. The doorkeeper has to bend low towards him, for the difference in height between them has altered much to the man's disadvantage. 'What do you want to know now?' asks the doorkeeper; 'you are insatiable'. 'Everyone strives to reach the Law', says the man, 'so how does it happen that for all these many years no one but myself has ever begged for admittance?' The doorkeeper recognises that the man has reached his end, and to let his failing senses catch the words roars in his ear: 'No one else could ever be admitted here, since this gate was made only for you. I am now going to shut it'. [62]

Like the character in this story, Joseph K inhabits a world which he cannot control, where decisions and systems dictate his fate. It is a world which he did not choose, but was born into, and yet is condemned to face the consequences.

In orthodox Christianity human beings are born into this world already guilty, already condemned, because of the so called 'fall' related in Genesis 3. Like Joseph K, they do not choose to be born, but have to face the consequences and responsibility for something they never chose. Because they are under judgement, God is entitled to end their lives at any moment, and indeed creates Hell

---

[62] Franz Kafka, 'Before the Law', www.mit.edu/norvinwww/something else/Kafka?html. (Accessed 24.9.2015)

to punish (eternally) those who don't accept His remedy to save humankind, namely the human blood- sacrifice of his innocent son.

We considered early on alternative understandings to Genesis 3, within broader considerations of evolutionary science, so I will not rehearse these arguments again. The reason why I am making reference to Joseph K's plight in *The Trial* is because it sums up much about the human condition as understood within a Judaeo-Christian context, where guilt, death, punishment are the tools by which religion is able to control and coerce, and the only way out is and acceptance of human sacrifice to appease the anger of God. God is all powerful and therefore demands worship. He is said to be in control of the universe, and able to intervene as He pleases.

Well, if this is truly the case, then He has an awful lot to answer for. So much suffering and cruelty have happened on his watch. The promise of future restoration does not cancel out the levels of suffering undergone by human beings down the centuries. If He had the ability to stop evil in its tracks, and did not, then his character must be called into question. The existentialists knew this. Nietzsche knew this.

Jean-Paul Sartre captures the agony of mind in an individual, which can inflict pain comparable to that of physical torture:

GARCIN: Open the door! Open, blast you! I'll endure anything, your red-hot tongs and molten lead, your racks and prongs and garrottes—all your fiendish gadgets, everything that burns and flays and tears—I'll out up with any torture you impose. Anything, anything would be better than this agony of mind, this creeping pain that gnaws and fumbles and caresses one and never hurts quite enough.[63]

For Sartre there is no benevolent God who enters into our suffering. For Sartre man is born by no choice of his own into a world of torturous pain and suffering. He has free will, and must bear the consequences of his choices alone. The choices of one individual always impact on others, as the play *No Exit* reminds us. For Sartre there is no loving God who understands human suffering. There is no compassionate God who has entered into suffering and gone through the pain of rejection and death in order to overcome it and point to a new hope.

In Lars Von Trier's film *Melancholia* protagonist Justine, who is suffering from catatonic depression and impending doom, as she has an inkling that the planet 'Melancholia' will collide with Earth, voices the tragedy of human condition which has echoed down the centuries: 'Life is only on earth, and not for long'.

Justine's words are of a universal nature, because they give voice to the angst that comes from recognising that human life is all that there is. The author of 2 Samuel expressed an analogous sentiment to that of Justine: 'We must all die; we are like water spilled on the ground, which cannot be gathered up again' (2 Samuel 14:14a).

It is a sentiment that goes back to beginning of human history. The writer of one of the most ancient Hebrew poetic texts voices the same existential reality: 'For we are but of yesterday and know nothing, for our days on earth are a shadow' (Job 8:9).

The irony is that both Jean Paul Sartre and Lars Von Trier as atheists echo the Hebrew poets and prophets of

---

[63] Jean Paul Sartre, *No Exit* (New York: vintage books, 1955), 42.

old. In *No Exit* the character. Inez states: 'You are—your life, and nothing else' (p.45).

Faith calls us to see further. To look at our world and believe that redemption and resurrection are possible. God calls us to open ourselves up to possibility, to the possibility that life can be different, not because difficult circumstances are vanished away, but because we can be transformed through love, and strengthened by hope.

In Albert Camus's novel *The Outsider*, the protagonist Meursault is visited by a priest in prison in the final part of the novel. Meursault is there because he murdered an Arab man. All his life Meursault has lived emotionally detached from the circumstances of his life. The novel opens at the death of his mother. He shows no emotion at her funeral. Meursault does not believe in God, nor does he seek to find comfort in anything, but faces the ordeal of living head on, with no desire for help from an outside source.

During the priest's visit to him whilst he is in prison, the priest tries to question his certainty about the existence of God. Meursault does not change his opinion. Whilst in the cell, the priest calls him to see deeper, to look at his surroundings through the eyes of faith. The priest says:

I know how the suffering oozes from these stones. I've never looked at them without a feeling of anguish. But deep in my heart I know that even the most wretched among you have looked at them and seen a divine face emerging from the darkness. It is that face which you are being asked to see.[64]

The priest is inviting Meursault to look deeper, to see further. It is a solicitation to see God in the midst of

---

[64] Albert Camus, *The Outsider*, translated by Joseph Laredo (London: Penguin Books, 1982), 113.

imprisonment, at the end of life itself. It is an invitation to open himself up to the possibility of God when life only seems like a theatre of the absurd.

Meursault gets increasing annoyed with the priest, and launches into a diatribe about the absurdity of existence.

Stepping back from the story, I have found that within my being there have two competing voices at times. There is the 'Meursault' within which causes me to despair at the world and the futility of it all, and which causes me to doubt God, and there is the voice of the priest, the call of faith to see further. This voice invites and calls me to see God at work in our world, despite the suffering and all of the questions. It calls me to throw myself into the mystery of God, which we can never really domesticate or comprehend although we can see: for it is a mystery embodied and known by love. There is a song we often sing which says 'Ubi caritas, et amor, Ubi caritas, Deus ibi est' which translates 'where there is love, there is God'.

One of the things that impresses me about Meursault is his refusal to comfort himself with the belief in a divine being who will put all things right. There is a bravery in his decision to confront his own predicament alone. But something within me also responds to what the priest says: daring to look around us and not simply see the stones of our prison cells, but to see God at work. This is not a belief in a God who will (or indeed can) wave a magic wand so that all pain and suffering disappear, which could happen in a fairy tale fantasy, but a God who is revealed in suffering, weakness and at times, absurdity ('For God's foolishness is wiser than human wisdom, and God's weakness is stronger than human strength [...] God chose what is foolish in the world to shame the wise; God chose what is weak in the world to shame the strong' [1 Corinthians 1: 25,27]).

There are aspects of Meursault's character that intrigue me and even inspire me, but aspects that don't. Like every existentialist hero, he faces his predicament without the comfort of a divine power who will sort everything out. But the flip side to this is that he is unable to be moved by the plight of others. Not only does he express no emotion at his mother's death, but kills an Arab man without any qualms. His emotional detachment enables him to face the consequences of life head on, but it does not allow him to show altruism, compassion or empathy, which lie at the very heart of what it means to be human. That is why when we see human beings who torture, kill and inflict pain we refer to them as having become dehumanised. Throughout history we have justified our violent and dehumanised tendencies by projecting them onto an image of God who is violent, who kills and throws into eternal hell all who do not accept him. In the Old Testament (as we have seen) much of our human violence and revenge is given justification 'in the name' (or as John Caputo would say 'under the name') of God.

Like a child who does not assume responsibility for his or her actions, we can paint a picture of God as the father up in the sky who will magic away all suffering and set the world to rights. But what if God is not all powerful? What if God did not create the world out of nothing, but that his first creative act was to bring light and order out of chaos? What if God is doing the best he can with the material he has to work with?

I know that this may sound deeply polemical and even heretical to some, but theologians will know that this kind of questioning has been around for a long time, and no one has articulated it as profoundly and powerfully as philosopher-theologian John Caputo.

For process theologians, God is all loving, but not all powerful. God did not create the universe *ex nihilo*, but is recreating it *ex nihilism* (for those of you wanting to follow this up in more detail, read Catherine Keller's book *On The Mystery: Discerning Divinity in Process*). The picture painted in Genesis 1 is that of God bringing hovering over the primordial waters, bringing created order and life; creation *ex profundis*, as she calls it.

For those reading this who have alarm bells ringing in their heads because they fear that Keller is departing from the Bible, think again: for her interpretation is deeply textual, and she engages with the biblical text in its original Hebrew to provide a radically new and inspiring interpretation. Reflecting on Genesis 1 she argues:

The narrative itself has long suffered from two kinds of interpretive absolutism. The literalist interpretations, unlike the Ambrosian allegory, reduce it to a bit of primitive pseudo-science. Then it lends itself to every form of religious war against secular science, whether the six-day creationism that simply junks the space time of astrophysics, or the more sophisticated 'intelligent design' campaign that tries understandably to resist neo-Darwinian reductionism but in doing so allies itself with the U.S. politics of fundamentalism.

Beyond the problems of biblical literalism, theology in general interprets the text as proof of God's creation of the world from absolutely nothing. Certainly the *creatio ex nihilo* is one possible interpretation of the text and of the universe. Both Testaments picture a creation through divine speech, a dramatic beginning of this universe rather than a static one or cyclical creation. Theologians rightly argue that the radical novelty and contingency of the creation—as creation, and not just inert eternal stuff—sets it off from a purposeless universe. Yet theology usually then presumes that the *ex nihilo* version of the creation is the only alternative to nihilism.

But something is fishy in the history of interpretation! For we learn from biblical scholars that the *ex nihilo* doctrine has no basis in the letter of the text itself. The Bible narrates instead various versions of a more mysterious process: that of creation from the deep, known as the watery chaos. It inspires an alternative both to the absolutes of a top-down, once-for-all act of creation—and to the dissolutes of mechanistic reductionism. The third was of an open-ended process of creation emerged in resistance to the presumption of a preprocessed creation. We may call this doctrinal alternative the *creatio ex profundis*.[65]

Keller's re-interpretation of the creation story of Genesis 1 is deeply biblical, but instead of setting up foundational axiomatic truths, Keller disrupts orthodoxy through what has become known as 'theopoetics'. Deeply influenced by the philosophers Gilles Deleuze & Felix Guattari, Keller sees the world as possibility, in which the spirit that hovered over the primordial waters is still at work, creating and recreating. Creation is therefore rescued from being understood as a one-off event, dropping from the sky *Deus ex machina*, but is a deeply incarnational process. Recreation is emphasised over creation, possibility and change over static dictats, the possibility for evolution and renewal is a dynamic presence which lies at the core of human life and the natural world.

In this theological paradigm, God is not an omnipotent figure in the sky, but is incarnated love down here. God is love, and opens up the possibility for love and reconciliation amidst the chaos and suffering which are a part of our world. God is present in Meursault's prison cell, but Meursault is blinded to him.

Throughout human history we have painted God in our image. We have projected the best and the worst of our

---

[65] Catherine Keller, *On The Mystery: Discerning Divinity in Process* (Minneapolis: Fortress Press, 2008), 47-48.

characteristics onto him. In the Old Testament we have the command to not kill alongside numerous commands to kill. We have the command to welcome the stranger alongside passages which command ethnic cleansing.

That is why the incarnation is needed. To clear up our confusion about God, and to see what love looks like in embodied form. The incarnation is a radical statement about what God is like, a culmination, an embodiment and enfleshment of the Godhead, revealing a God who is not all powerful, but all loving. We must not be confused here. To claim that God is not all powerful does not mean that he does not have power. Jesus healed the sick, raised the dead, walked on water and fed the multitudes. He had power, but his power was manifested through love.

The power of love and forgiveness can transform our world, because love can change the human heart from coldness, hatred, pride and indifference, to compassion, empathy, humility and grace.

In his recent book *The Insistence of God: A Theology of Perhaps*, John Caputo argues: 'God as a Highest Being—a steady hand at the wheel of the universe, ordering all things to good purpose, the spanning providential eye overseeing all—has had a good run'. [66] Drawing more heavily on Jacques Derrida rather than Deleuze & Guattari as Catherine Keller does, Caputo has had a long quest to uncover what lies under the name of God, or in his words, what is the 'event' that is harboured by that name. Deconstruction enables him to strip away the facade of language, open it up to its complexity and possibility, and in the process dismantle (deconstruct) fixed notions which we may have about God. Although he is not a process

---

[66] John Caputo, *The Insistence of God: A Theology of Perhaps* (Indiana Series in the Philosophy of Religion. Bloomington & Indianapolis: Indiana University Press, 2013), Kindle edition loc. 60-61.

theologian, as a philosopher he shares some common ground with Keller in not seeing God as an all-powerful outsider. Caputo argues:

> The world is neither a neat, divinely run cosmos nor pure chaos but what James Joyce called so prophetically 'chaosmos', a dance of probabilities sometimes producing improbable results. That fits with biblical creation: in the Beginning, at the time God was creating the world, the elements were already there, as old as God. The Bible begins with a B (bet, *bereshit*) not an A (aleph). The first is already invaded by the second (just as 'deconstruction' would predict).[67]

Many Christians are uncomfortable when French philosopher Derrida is cited, and especially when they see the word 'deconstruction'. But this fear is unfounded, for at its core Derrida's idea of deconstruction basically relates to the possibilities of language, as well as its limitations. Deconstruction militates against closed readings of texts, readings that lock the possibilities of interpretation down. It is diametrically opposed to fundamentalist approaches to a text, which essentially claim that there is only one correct interpretation of a given text. Deconstruction opens the text up, and enables us to see the text in all its possibilities. The text has the power to disrupt, disturb, challenge and correct our tendencies to monopolise the interpretive process. Deconstruction finds it *raison d'être* on the margins rather than in the established centre, which is why it can never be the language of conquest or empire. It distrusts those who use language to justify power and violence, and always demands that the reader be humble in his or her interpretation, as the text always has more to say.

I understand the function of deconstruction as very close to that of the Spirit, which always challenges,

---

[67] Caputo, *The Insistence of God*, loc 62-63.

disturbs, renews and re-creates. When I use the word 'disturb' I do so not as a negative term, but in the sense of 'stirring', or 'agitating' as used in the context of John 5:4 when the man is healed at the pool of Bethesda. You will recall the story of how the blind, the lame and the paralysed would wait by the pool and when the Angel of The Lord came and stirred up the troubled the waters, they would go into the pool and be healed. Jesus encounters a man who had been waiting at the pool for 38 years, because nobody would help him into the water. Jesus heals him by the power of his word.

Deconstruction acts like the Angel on the waters. It disrupts, disturbs and troubles the surface, opening up new possibilities which can bring healing and liberation. I quote now from the King James Version because I prefer the translation/interpretation of this particular verse:

> For an angel went down at a certain season into the pool, and troubled the water: whosoever then first after the troubling of the water stepped in was made whole of whatsoever disease he had. (John 5:4)

Just like the Spirit hovering over the waters of chaos at the beginning of time, the work of the Spirit continues to disrupt, disturb and open up new creative ways for healing and life.

Deconstruction works in a similar way, because it does not allow us to become fixated with the pool of water always being the same, but always disrupts the surface appearance of the world to take us deeper. At times this is risky and uncomfortable for us, because we feel safer on the surface level where everything appears too familiar. But for real healing and transformation, we must be like the lame and paralysed in John 5, who dare to be plunged into the waters of possibility, from where life, healing and liberation can come.

So when we read of passages in the Old Testament, where 'God' orders the annihilation of all men, women and children (for example 1 Samuel 15:3 which reads 'Now go and attack Amalek, and utterly destroy all that they have; do not spare them, but kill both man and woman, child and infant, ox and sheep, camel and donkey'), this terrible genocide is justified in 'the name of God', as an act of obedience to him.

But we need to ask ourselves the question: 'when something terrible is done in the name of God, what does the word "God" harbour'? We need to reject the surface interpretation of the word 'God'. We needs to deconstruct and ask questions of the text. Are the writers and editors of the biblical texts using the name of God to justify acts of violence? Are they projecting onto God their own lust for power, domination and violence?

The name of God, as Caputo has suggested, always harbours an event: the event on this occasion, is man's brutal violence towards his fellow man, not 'God'. The word 'God' in this text does not point to a stable idea of a transcendent being, but to their own particular understanding (mis-understanding) of what God was like, and what he demanded.

Contrast the 'event' beneath the word 'God' in the earlier passage in Deuteronomy 10:19, which harbours an altogether different event under the same name: 'You shall also love the stranger, therefore, for you were strangers in the land of Egypt'.

Why is all of this relevant to a chapter which is about 'broken God'? Because understanding the way in which language works, the way in which language shapes and constructs our world, has huge implications for how we read texts, and especially a sacred text, like the Bible. It allows us to see how a name can become a justification for atrocities, because it harbours an event, not a stable meaning. Deconstruction dismantles fossilised interpretations. It unmasks the illusion that the text only offers one interpretation. It challenges us to wait for the Spirit to disrupt the waters, asking of us that we do not accept things at face value, but always open ourselves up for the possibilities of delving deeper, for it is when we plunge into the waters where we find healing. This is similar to the symbolism of baptism, where life and renewal comes from being immersed or sprinkled with the water that disrupts the status quo, and reminds us that we are birthed into the community of faith, the waters of a new birth which cleanse, nourish and heal.

Much of the violence we see today at the hands of Islamist extremists is because they approach their own sacred texts literally and un-problematically. They take certain verses of the Qur'an, read them through a literalist lens which takes no account of the context in which the texts first emerged, and use them as a justification for their murderous crimes. This could never happen if they were to embrace deconstruction as a reading tool. By the way, I am not suggesting that we solve the problems of Isis by getting them to read Jacques Derrida! I realise that this may not be widely seen as viable strategy, but I think you get my point. Namely, that deconstruction needs to be understood as a force for good, and not negatively (as has been the case in most religious circles). You cannot build dictatorships of terror (whether divine or human) by appealing to the words of a tyrant, if you encompass those words within the framework of deconstruction.

The added issue faced by Muslims *vis-à-vis* The Qur'an, when compared to Christians with The Bible or Judaism with The Torah, is the way in which The Qur'an views itself (so to speak). It sees itself as the revealed word of the prophet, transcribed, dictated and written down. However, when you open the Bible, there is an open foregrounding of the fact that what we are dealing with are a collection of books of very different genres, written and redacted by hundreds of different human agents, spanning thousands of years, in very different contexts. Such a structure of texts militates against fundamentalist readings, because what we obviously are dealing with is a polyphony of myriad voices, not one.

This need not dilute what we understand as divine inspiration. It just depends whether you think that God can communicate truth through a myriad of different voices at different times, which I believe He can.

In my opinion modern-day Islam needs deconstructing. It needs reformation from within. Islamist extremist terrorism will not be defeated by military might, but only from within, when those who revere and live by the words of the Qur'an are able to deconstruct them, to see them for what they are, and to move away from any fixed illusions about how texts operate. Of course, I am not suggesting that Derrida is the panacea for defeating Islamic extremism! But how religious communities engage with their 'sacred texts' is more important in today's world than ever before.

Modern day Islam needs its own organically grown version of 'process theology'.

Process theologian John B. Cobb Jr and David Ray Griffin argue:

The term 'process' rightly suggests that this movement rejects static actuality and affirms that all actuality is process [...]

Process thought by definition affirms that process is fundamental. It does not assert that *everything* is in process; for that would mean that even the fact that things are in process is subject to change. There are in changing principles of process and abstract forms. But to be *actual* is to be a process. Anything which is not a process is an abstraction from process, not a full-fledged actuality' [...]

The bare assertion that the actual is processive has religious significance even by itself. Since the world as we experience it is a place of process, of change, of becoming, of growth and decay, the contrary notion that what is actual or fully real is being change leads to a devaluation of life in the world. Since our basic religious drive is to be in harmony with the fully real, belief that the fully real is beyond process encourages one or another form of escape from full participation in the world. But to understand that the process is the reality directs the drive to be 'with it' into immersion in the process.

The religious implication of reality as processive is in harmony with one of the chief consequences of the Judeo-Christian vision of reality. In this tradition, God has been viewed as active within the historical process. Accordingly, historical activity has had more importance than in traditions without a doctrine of the purposive-providential presence of the sacred reality in history. Those cultures decisively affected by the Judaeo-Christian view owe to it much of their vitality.[68]

Process theology is polemical to many traditionalists because it deconstructs and dislodges our conceptions of an all-powerful and omniscient God, seated up in heaven, and ultimately controlling history. It takes the rug from under our feet, and in a sense demands more faith, because the certainties we once had have now been swept away. As Caputo has inferred, instead of certainty there is a call, a solicitation, a promise, and invitation to believe... When we respond to that call, something happens. Faith, mingled with prayer and hope begin to transform us, causing us to look beyond ourselves, to transcend our

---

[68] John B. Cobb Jr., & David Ray Griffin, *Process Theology: An. Introductory Exposition* (Philadelphia: The Westminster Press, 1976), 7, 14.

individualism and to love for others, which is to live for God.

We plunge into the watery chaos of life (reminiscent of the *tehom*, the depths in Genesis 1), now questioning whether it is God who has created that chaos, but believing that God is the presence of light and love, bringing beauty and the possibilities of life, out of the murky waters of despair.

We are carried by hope, led by love, drawn by a word, into the abyss of God's recreating grace, which births a new community of faith who love God, not for the promise or certainty of an afterlife, not in the safe knowledge that all will be out right; but being transformed through love in the midst of the daily, existential, struggle of faith and doubt.

This does not mean that we stop believing in the afterlife. Christ's resurrection from the dead proclaims the death of death, and ushers in bold hope that sin, death and decay will not have the final word. But we do not live for the afterlife. We live in and for the present, prayerfully crying out for our lives and our world to be changed through love. Allowing our lives to be transformed by the love of God, so that there is no place in our hearts for greed, pride, hatred, violence and war.

Our world will not be changed by politicians and politics alone. Power always ends up favouring the strong. It always follows the interests of business and the markets. This is true for right-wing governments as much as left wing. Left-wing governments on the whole may invest more in health, education and the poor, but ultimately they will be limited in what they can do, because they need to court big businesses and the financial markets, and these do not have human welfare as their priorities.

Human beings are only worth as much as their market value, as both consumers and workers. Human beings are treated as commodities.

Neither left or right will change the global structures of injustice. They would be voted out by their electorates. To change the structural injustices of the world demands giving up of wealth, resources, and power, and no government is prepared to do that. At the end of the day we all struggle with selfishness and greed. We are all subject to fear. And if we were to be placed in a situation where the well-being and access to resources we enjoy in the developed countries were to be taken away, how soon would we begin to hate, scapegoat and kill to protect what we have?

It is the mission and role of the church to show a different way. Every church should have as its mission statement the Sermon on the Mount, which if we were to embrace and enact, would wipe out all war, injustice and hunger. And it would do so not through coercive power, but through the power of love, which although is weak when contrasted with power, is strong.

The God of peace, revealed in Christ, comes not in the power of military and political might, but in weakness. But it is through this association with the poor, the outcast and the needy, that the kingdoms of God is established. We are called to do the same. We are called to be renewed and changed by the love of Christ.

Ghandi meditated on the Sermon on the Mount everyday. If we were to do so collectively as the church, our world would be changed:

Blessed are the poor in spirit, for theirs is the kingdom   of heaven.
Blessed are those who mourn, for they will be comforted.

Blessed are the meek, for they will inherit the earth.

Blessed are those who hunger and thirst for righteousness, for they will be filled.
Blessed are the merciful, for they will receive mercy.
Blessed are the pure in heart, for they will see God.
Blessed are the peacemakers, for they will be called the children of God.

Blessed are those who are persecuted for righteousness' sake, for theirs is the kingdom of heaven. (Matthew 5: 3-11)

The Sermon on the Mount is counter-cultural and counter intuitive. It calls for us to respond and resist in ways which are contrary to our human nature. It militates against the Darwinian impulse within us all for self-preservation. It also boldly asserts that it is the meek, not the powerful who will inherit the earth. It is those who use force and military might, not the merciful, who dictate foreign policy. And there are very few 'children of God', if being a child of God means being a peacemaker.

And very few of us would be willing to be persecuted for righteousness sake. Of course many of our Christian brothers and sisters across the globe are doing living out the reality of this, as they are tortured, imprisoned and killed for their faith. But for those of us living in the West, this is a distant reality.

We live in a world which is contrary to this. The strong in spirit are those who wield control. The powerful and the strong are the ones who control the world's resources, not the meek.

Jesus embodied the Sermon on the Mount fully. His death was 'for righteousness sake'. He lived a life given over to the meek, the poor, the broken-hearted, the sick and the lame. He stood with the outsider and refused to fight the imperial cruelties of Rome through violence, and in so doing ushered in the kingdom of heaven.

And we are called to do the same.
But if we are honest with ourselves, we don't.

This is one of the reasons why the church is in decline in the western world.

We do not truly believe, embrace and live out the Sermon on the Mount, and as it warns us only a few verses later in this same passage, when the salt has lost its taste it is no longer good for anything, and when a light is hidden, then it brings benefit to no one:

You are the salt of the earth; but if the salt has lost its taste, how can its saltiness be restored? It is no longer good for anything, but is thrown out and trampled underfoot.
You are the light of the world. A city built on a hill cannot be hidden. No one after lighting a lamp puts it under the bushel basket, but on the lamp stand, and it gives light to all in the house. In the same way, let your light shine before others, so that they may see your good works and give glory to your Father in heaven. (Matthew 5: 13-16)

If the global church were truly to embrace and embody the Sermon on the Mount, it would regain its prophetic voice in our world.

The reason why much of the church is in decline is because it is not following the teachings of the one it claims to follow. It has become too accommodated with the structures that dominate our society. It hasn't preached a radical message of hope and change. It has too easily capitulated to patterns and mind-sets of the society in which it lives, rather than proclaiming and living by the Sermon on the Mount.

If the church is to have a future, it will need to embrace the cause of the poor in a far more radical way. Its mission will need to be directed towards challenging the structural evil we are a part of, denouncing violence and greed, fear and self-preservation, and aligning itself not with the powerful of this world, but the meek.

God is most fully revealed in Jesus Christ, whose power is shown in a life poured out in the service of others, bringing healing and reconciliation wherever he went. A power revealed in being able to live according to a different principle to the ruling political and religious authorities of the day. The power to go into the wilderness and to be tempted by the devil, who offered him earthly power (the kingdoms of this world), the quick satisfaction of all his needs (stones turned into bread) and a religious trump card that believed in a God was there to intervene and sweep him up (throw yourself off the high place and the angels will rescue you).

Much of our modern day religion has bowed to these self-same temptations of Christ in the wilderness, for we have used our faith to bring us material well-being, power, and a belief in an all-powerful God who can swoop down at any time and rescue us. Such capitalistic conceptions of faith did not sit well with our Messiah. He knew that the only way in which the power of God could be revealed was in resisting the easy options offered by Satan. He knew that the transformative power of God could only be realised when he became weakened by denying what would have been an easy way out, but remaining in that place of prayer and in the wilderness where he was to be emptied of every human vestige of prestige, wealth, power, and a belief in God as a crutch (as Freud would have it) who could rescue him at any turn.

By refusing the easy comfort offered to him by the devil, but remaining faithful to his inner call, though his physical body became weakened and emaciated from hunger, and his mind emptied by isolation and loneliness, with only the desert sky and silence as his companion, power was being perfected in weakness. The preparation for what he would go through on the cross was being forged in the fires of suffering and daily struggle.

He would defeat the devil in the wilderness, and he would defeat him again at the cross.

Resurrection and reconciliation would come in his refusal to bow to the allures and easy way out offered by Satan.

In showing love towards his enemies, in remaining true to his cause to change the world through healing love, and show us the only way in which God can transform our world, in subverting our misguided notions of how God worked; he changed history into a before and after.

The early church was to be established on his example. Whatever your beliefs are on the resurrection, whether you believe in a physical resurrection or a symbolic one: something radical happened. Something transformative in history happened, for the apostles and followers of Christ were emboldened to face their accusers head on, and to die for their faith, in the hope that they would rise to life.

The early church refused to combat Rome with violence, but became a community (as we are told of in the book of Acts) where a radical new way of living was made possible. Possessions were shared, people were healed of their aliments and brought into the family of believers, and the world was transformed.

It is said that Rome was converted to Christianity from its pagan religions because of the testimony of the Christian martyrs, sent to their death in thousands, crucified, burnt alive, thrown to wild beasts, persecuted and chased into the catacombs where they were living, and yet not retaliating in kind, not repaying evil for evil, but following the example of Christ, in the hope that he had defeated the power and fear of death. This self-sacrificial and outpoured love always brings reconciliation, it always brings resurrection and hope for our world, and for our communities. And we are called to do the same.

We too are invited to answer and respond to the call.

Julie Beausobre, whose husband had died in the death camps of Stalin (where she also endured torture and isolation), was asked how she managed to survive the gulag. She responded:

It was simple really. I tried to love my torturers, because if I loved them I would not be adding to the evil in the world, and they would not have succeeded in adding to the evil in the world by making me hate them.

But if I loved, it could just be that it might have some effect on them and even reduce the evil in the world. At its simplest level Christ's way of love and trust and forgiveness seemed to be the only way.[69]

---

[69] Julia De Beausobre, *The Woman Who Could Not Die* (London: Chatto & Windus, 1938), 52.

Chapter 6

Gender God[70]

Few would contest that the Bible has been used to subjugate women. Projections of God (who is spirit, and therefore neither male nor female) were always going to be in the masculine, given the historical context in which the biblical texts were written. (His)story is usually written by the strong and the dominant, and patriarchy has had an almost free run of history until the second half of the 19th century, when the women's rights and suffragist movements began to emerge. In the Western tradition, we are indebted to the so-called first wave of feminism, which was dominated by Virginia Woolf (1882-1941) and Simone de Beauvoir (1908-1986). Virginia Woolf's extended fictional essay *A Room of One's Own* (1929) examines the historical subjugation of women in the field of literature, and invents the character of 'Judith Shakespeare', making the point that had Shakespeare had a sister gifted with similar literary talents to himself, there is no way in which she would have been able to flourish in the society of the day, as women's creativity and ambition were given no room within the patriarchal structures:

> I could not help thinking, as I looked at the works of Shakespeare on the shelf, that the bishop was right at least in

[70] I am not discussing same sex relations in this chapter. This is not because I deem it a controversial subject that I want to avoid, but simply because of space. I am pro LGBT, and critical of any theological approach that serves to perpetuate the traditional denunciation of any particular gender. I am fully in agreement with Steve Chalke, and I highly recommend his article 'The Bible and Homosexuality: Part One', which can be found at the following web address: **https://www.premierchristianity.com/Featured-Topics/Homosexuality/The-Bible-and-Homosexuality-Part-One**

(accessed 20.9.2016)

this; it would have been impossible, completely and entirely, for any woman to have written the plays of Shakespeare in the age of Shakespeare. Let me imagine, since facts are so hard to come by, what would have happened had Shakespeare had a wonderful gifted sister, called Judith [...]?[71]

Simone de Beauvoir's most famous book, *The Second Sex* (1949) distinguished between sex and gender. Sex is biologically determined, whereas gender is socially constructed. This led her to claim that one is not born a woman, but becomes one:

> Woman is determined not by her hormones or mysterious instincts, but by the manner in which her body and her relation to the world are modified through the action of others than herself. The abyss that separates the adolescent boy and girl has been deliberately opened between them since earliest childhood; later on, woman could be other than what she *was made*, and that past was bound to shadow her for life. If we appreciate its influence, we see clearly that her destiny is not predetermined for all eternity.[72]

The so-called Second Wave of feminists emerged during the revolutionary 1960s, when western traditional societal structures were being challenged across the board, in politics, literature, music and medicine (the advent of the contraceptive pill etc). Intellectual giants such as Julia Kristeva (1941-), Helen Cixous (1937-), Luce Irigary (1932-) and many others, challenged male dominated discourse and philosophy by deconstructing and getting under the skin of language and history, to show how language, discourse, law and the power structures enable society to function, are dominated by patriarchal ideology. Through a re-examination of ancient myths, in addition to

---

[71] Virginia Woolf, *A Room of One's Own*, edited with and introduction by Morag Shiach (Oxford: Oxford U.P., 1992), 60.
[72] Simone de Beauvoir, *The Second Sex*, translated and edited by H.M. Parshley (London: Everyman's Library, 1993), 760.

important 20th century figures such as Freud and Lacan, these feminist theorists showed-up what I will metaphorically refer to as 'the patriarchal scaffolding'; by which I mean, the structures which are no longer visible once the edifice has been erected (pun intended), but which are foundational for understanding how it was constructed in the first place. In questioning how language, societal norms, social spaces, culture, literature, professions etc are cut through by ideological dominance, these theorists were able to question and subvert its very foundations, and open up liberatory 'lines of flight' (to coin a phrase of French philosopher Gilles Deleuze), that is to say, ways out (and new ways in) to language, discourse, and power.

It is not my intention to provide a history of feminism in the space of this chapter. Nor is it to provide a history of significant women within Scripture, on which volumes have already been written. Rather, it is to briefly reference the liberatory aspects of Scripture in terms of gender emancipation, in the hope of showing that whilst the Bible has been used historically to undermine women, it also constitutes one of the most liberatory texts in terms of gender equality and emancipation.

We need to understand why the word 'God', has become associated with masculine qualities, when The Bible clearly teaches that God is spirit (neither masculine of feminine), and God is love (1 John 4:8 'Anyone who does not love does not know God, because God is love'). Love, by its very own definition, considers the other as better, and cannot coerce and control: 'There is no fear in love, but perfect love casts out fear. For fear has to do with punishment, and whoever fears has not been perfected in love' (1 John 4:18). As John Caputo has explored in much of his work, the name of God harbours an event. And the name of God has been used to impose certain societal structures, to fossilise certain religious beliefs, and to promote certain ideas about God, as an all-powerful figure 'up there', controlling history and its final denouément.

I have heard some argue from within the Christian tradition, 'very well, God is spirit, neither male or female, but does the incarnation not show that God is male, I mean, is God becoming a man not proof of this?'. But what if we were to turn this argument on its head for a moment, and consider that perhaps the reason why God became man was not about reinforcing patriarchal structures, but precisely the opposite? Maybe patriarchy needed to be liberated from within, by showing us an example of what true manhood should look like? Maybe the only way in which the history of abuse, control and exclusion of women, could be brought about by God incarnating as man, to free manhood of their enslavement to patriarchal structures, boldly stating that Christ is our example and model, and the one who can save us from ourselves, from our propensity to subdue, control and exert our will over the other?

Christ, touched by the 'unclean woman' in Luke 8:40-48,[73] Christ in the home of Mary and Martha, with whom

---

[73] Now when Jesus returned, the crowd welcomed him, for they were all waiting for him. And there came a man named Jairus, who was a ruler of the synagogue. And falling at Jesus' feet, he implored him to come to his house, for he had an only daughter, about twelve years of age, and she was dying.

As Jesus went, the people expressed around him. And there was a woman who had had a discharge of blood for twelve years, and though she had spent all her living on physicians, and she could not be healed by anyone. She came up behind him and touched the fringe of his garment, and immediately her discharge of blood ceased. And Jesus said, 'Who was it that touched me?' When all denied it, Peter said, 'Master, the crowds surround you and are pressing in on you!" But Jesus said, 'Someone touched me, for I perceive that power has gone out from me.' And when the woman saw that she was not hidden, she came trembling, and falling down before him he was good friends, Christ's deep relationship with Mary Magdalene; all attest to the dignity and affection with which he treated women. Mary Magdalene showed more courage and loyalty then many of Jesus's disciples, who fled at his crucifixion because of the associated shame and risk to them as followers. Peter, as we know, denied him three times, claiming that 'he never knew him'. Not so with Mary Magdalene. She accompanied Jesus to the end. She was there at the crucifixion, and also at the resurrection, which should give her the status of an apostle (Matthew 27:56 & Matthew 27:61). It is easy to gloss over these well-known verses, and miss the startling implications of them. In Matthew 27:56 it states that Mary Magdalene was one of those who was 'ministering' to Jesus. In his hour of weakness, and yet in his hour of incredible strength and courage, God the Son is ministered to. And by a woman. Not just any woman, but one who had been an outcast on the fringes of society, possessed with seven demons until they are cast out of her by Jesus, as recorded in Luke 8:1-2.[74] Then, following the resurrection, it is Mary Magdalene who, according to the gospel of John, announces to the disciples '"I have seen the Lord"' (John 20:18). Seeing the risen Lord was what would later confer you the title of 'apostle'. In many churches today, the title 'apostle' is banded about and given liberally to many within the church, but this represents a severe departure from the New Testament definition of what apostle means. In Acts 1:21, when the disciples are seeking to find a replacement for Judas as apostle, it is stated very clearly that whoever

---

declared in the presence of all the people why she had touched him, and how she had been immediately healed. And he said to her, 'Daughter, your faith has made you well; go in peace.'

[74] 'Soon afterward he went on through cities and villages, proclaiming and bringing the good news of the kingdom of God. And the twelve were with him, and also some women who had been healed of evil spirits and infirmities: Mary, called Magdalene, from whom seven demons had gone out'.

was appointed would have to had witnessed the risen Saviour.[75] Paul also clearly states this qualification in 1 Corinthians 9:1 when he says 'Am I not free? Am I not an apostle? Have I not seen Jesus our Lord?'

Mary Magdalene's waiting by the cross, and waiting by the tomb, has often been glossed over in church tradition, or been subjected to little more than crass sentimentality. For me, it represents an all-important event. It is a paradigm changer, for it sets a woman as witness to the two key events in the whole of history. But there is much more to it than this. There are so many implications from what is left unsaid about Mary Magdalene, given the schematic brush strokes of the verses where she is mentioned in the Gospels at the time of the crucifixion and resurrection. The mere fact that she was present, is proof of both her courage and loyalty to Christ, as in being there when so many other of Jesus's closest disciples had fled the scene, would have put her life at risk.

Although biblical references to Mary Magdalene could fit onto one page of the Bible, their presence disrupts, subverts, and dignifies not only the human condition, but particularly womankind. Given the imposed invisibility of women down the centuries, the 'Magdalene passages' (as I will refer to them from now on) represent an epiphany. An event of real significance and transcendence beyond the

---

[75] 'So one of the men who have accompanied us during all the time that the Lord Jesus went in and out among us, beginning from the baptism of John until the day when she was taken up from us—one of these men must become with us a witness to his resurrection.' And they put forward two, Joseph called Barsabbas, who was also called Justus, and Matthias. And they prayed and said, 'You, Lord, who know the hearts of all, show which one of these two you have chosen to take the place in this ministry and apostleship from which Judas turned aside to go to his own place.' And they cast lots for them, and the lot fell on Matthias, and he was numbered with the eleven apostles.'

historically contingent. Her witness of the crucified and risen Christ is not to be understood as passive observation, but of committed devotion to a person, and a message, that she was prepared to stand by and live by, even in the face of shame, neglect, danger, doubt, and eventual surprise and hope. Her presence at these cosmic moments in history, place her in a category not even achieved by the twelve disciples. And the fact that the editors and redactors alluded to her, is of significance in itself.

What I am wanting to suggest is that whilst the Bible has been used to oppress and subjugate women, it can be read differently, in terms of liberation and human dignity, even if church history has typically projected an image of God anthropomorphised into a patriarchal being.

Mary Daly, arguably one of the most important feminist theologians of the 20th century, sets out the issue as follows:

The biblical and popular image of God as a great patriarch in heaven, rewarding and punishing according to his mysterious and seemingly arbitrary will, has dominated the imagination of millions over thousands of years. The symbol of the Father God, spawned in the human imagination and sustained as plausible by patriarchy, has in turn rendered service to this type of society by making its mechanisms for the oppression of women appear right and fitting. If God in 'his' heaven is a father ruling 'his' people, then it is the 'nature' of things and according to divine plan and the order of the universe that society be male-dominated.[76]

We have seen in previous chapters how Process Theology, in conjunction with Deconstruction and post-structuralist philosophy, has brought about radical new

---

[76] Mary Daly, *Beyond God the Father: Towards a Philosophy of Women's Liberation* (London: The Women's Press, 1973), 13.

readings of sacred scripture, which although may be challenging and polemical to traditionalists, are liberatory and emancipatory. The act of re-engaging and re-interpreting scripture is crucial for disrupting fossilised fundamentalism. Jesus engaged with it more than most, when he would say ' Moses taught you....' But 'I say....' Or, 'it was said of old....' 'But I say to you....'. The church which I form a part of has at its core the belief of renewal and reform. A church that isn't reforming is one that eventually dies.

It is proof of the dominance of patriarchal mindset that the apostle Paul has been remembered more for being against women than for them. How is it, that he has largely been remembered for the verse (1 Corinthians 14:34) which instructs women to 'be silent in church'; rather than for the incredible paradigm shifting words of Galatians 3:28, which reads: 'There is neither Jew nor Greek, there is neither slave nor free, there is no male or female, for you are all one in Christ'?

The verse which instructs women to be silent is contextual, specific to a certain situation which had arisen in the church in Corinth. It was not a universal statement, and never intended as such. It is just that it has served patriarchy to treat it that way, whilst ignore the bold, universal a moment of epiphany in Galatians 3:28, which is about breaking down the walls of division and exclusion which we construct. It is about the liberatory power of God's love which militates against our propensity to exclude, put down, and dominate one particular group, because we believe ourselves to be superior. These words of Paul are truly transformational and utterly unique, given the context he was living in. Why has one verse of Paul's been prioritised over another? What is also curious, is that most of the literalists (although not all) have not completely subscribed to 1 Corinthians 14:34, as they have allowed women to pray or read the scripture in church. Once again we are back to what we looked at some chapters ago, whereby even the literalists don't follow their own advice regarding how Scripture is to be read: they too make decisions about what to read and how to read it.

At the same time, why has Galatians 3:28 been largely ignored?

We need an ethical framework when we approach Scripture, recognising that God uses scripture to reveal Christ and his Word, and it therefore has real value and is inspired, but this does not detract from the constant need to test everything we read against how it measures up to love. Jesus himself read the Old Testament this way. He deliberately associated himself with the suffering servant in the second Isaiah, never with the ethnic cleansers and warriors of old. This represented a definite, ethical choice.

One of Judith Butler's many books is entitled *Antigone's Claim: Kinship Between Life and Death*.[77] What is significant about this book, is that it focuses on the character of Antigone, who was the daughter of Oedipus and Jocasta (Oedipus' mother). One of Butler's questions relates what we choose to focus on, and the ripple effects this has on wider culture. This is articulated with direct reference to Oedipus and Antigone. The Oedipus Myth, as we know, has informed much of 20th century psychology and philosophy, as it was the basis for Freud's work on sexuality and the unconscious, and then taken up by Lacan, Kristeva, Zizek and many more. You will have all heard of the so-called 'Oedipus complex', at the heart of Freud's theory about how male and female identities are shaped.

[77] Judith Butler, *Antigone's Claim: Kinship Between Life and Death* (New York: Columbia University Press, 2000).

It is not my intention to go into this in much detail here. All I am interested in doing is to draw attention to Butler's question, that had we focussed and adopted Antigone rather than Oedipus as a foundational character upon whom to build philosophy and psychology, how would have that changed things?

Translating this question into the context of the Bible, we could ask a similar question: if the mark of an apostle was to have witnessed the risen Christ, how would have it changed the course of history had Mary Magdalene been made an apostle? (She also showed more courage and commitment than many of Jesus' closest disciples, remaining at the cross when most had fled, and when Peter had denied him three times).

What we read, and how we read, always has huge implications, and therefore always involves an ethical choice. We need to read the Bible through the lens of the oppressed, which includes women, and allow it to shape our theology and practice.

But let's get back to the intriguing figure of Antigone for a few moments. As stated earlier, she is the product of an incestuous relationship between Oedipus and his mother Jocasta. Antigone is a character who shows great courage, bravery and dignity, which puts her life at real risk. Basically, she is punished by being locked in a tomb, after attempting to bury her brother Polynices in a dignified way, which was prohibited by the laws of the city of Thebes. It is a story about power and who should succeed, because after Oedipus dies, the brother of Jocasta (Creon) sees himself as the next in line to the throne. Fratricidal violence breaks out between Polynices and his brother Eteocles, who were supposed to rule by taking it in turns. They kill each other, and whilst Eteocles is given a dignified burial, Polynices (by order of Creon) is prohibited from having a burial, and his corpse is left to decay and be eaten by wild animals. The reason why Enteocles is favoured by Creon over his brother Polynices, is because Enteocles had remained faithful and subject the the law of Thebes, whereas Polynices had left from under the city's jurisdiction, to form an army with which to fight his brother. Polynices is considered a traitor and enemy thereafter.

After burying her brother herself, she is locked up in a tomb and hangs herself. Her tragic end points to the suffering of countless women down the centuries whose lives have been cruelly ended and brought short, in the face of great suffering, exclusion and violence. There is a sense with Antigone that her manner of death (suicide) militates against passive acceptance of circumstance, as she takes her own fate into her hands. However we interpret and read this, there is no question that her brave actions in giving her brother a dignified burial in the face of male cruelty, violence and fratricide, sets her apart and places her on a different ethical plane to those around her. She openly resists and defies the patriarchal rules of her time, but tragically will end up paying for them with her own life.

When Creon says to her 'An enemy is not a friend, even when dead', Antigone responds 'I cannot share their hate, only their love'.

Later in the play, her defiance against the male dominated power structures leads Creon to banish her from the city:

CREON: I shall take her down some wild, desolate path never trod by men, and wall her up alive in a rocky vault, and set out short rations, just the measure piety demands to keep the entire city free of defilement. There let her pray to the one god she worships: Death—who knows?—may just reprieve her from death. Or she may learn at last, better late than never, what a waste of breath it is to worship Death.[78]

Antigone's courage and ethical stance comes at great personal cost. Her imprisonment and banishment from society is symbolic of the exclusion and oppression of women down the centuries. In one of the climactic scenes of the play, Antigone gives voice to her predicament, fully aware that she would rather suffer the cruelty and exclusion of her current fate, then to have never honoured her brother's death. In her own words she is 'going alive into the depths of the dead':

> O tomb, my bridal-bed—my house, my prison
> cut in the hollow rock, my everlasting watch!
> I'll be there, soon embrace my own,
> the great growing family of our dead
> Persephone has received among her ghosts.
>
> I, the last of them all, the most reviled by far,
> Go down before my destined time's run out.
> But still I go, cherishing one good hope:
> my arrival may be dear to father,
> dear to you my mother,
> dear to you, my loving brother, Eteocles—
>
> When you died I washed you with my hands,
> I dressed you all, I poured the sacred cups
> across your tombs. But now, Polynices,
> because I laid your body out as well,
> this, this is my reward. Nevertheless
> I honoured you—the decent will admit it—
> well and wisely too.[79]

---

[78] Sophocles, *Antigone*. In *The Three Thebian Plays: Antigone, Oedipus the King, Oedipus at Colonus*, translated by Robert Fagles (London: Penguin, 1984), 54-128 (p.100)
[79] Sophocles, *Antigone*, 105.

Written before 441 BC, Sophocles' *Antigone* foreshadows aspects of Christ's journey to the cross. Just as Antigone is punished for doing what is right, Christ is rejected and accused for being a friend of sinners. Antigone stands up against the moral codes of the day, following a deeper ethic that elicits anger in the society at the time. Christ subverts the moral code of the Pharisees and Sadducees, by calling for a religion that is less obsessed with outward moral codes and more about compassion.

Both Antigone and Christ engage wilfully in their bold acts of civil disobedience in the full knowledge that they may be punished. This does not stop them from following what they believe to be right, but only serves strengthen their resolve.

Antigone stands out as an early example of a woman who defies the unjust patriarchal norms of the day. She shows great courage and ethical determination to face imprisonment and exclusion for doing what it right.

It is not only in Greek tragedy that we find examples of notable women who have risked their lives for doing what is right. In the 'genealogy' of Jesus, as recorded in The Gospel according to Mathew, five women are mentioned: Tamar, Rahab, Ruth, Bathsheba (referred to in verse 6 as 'wife of Uriah') , and Mary. Of course, by implication many more feature elliptically in the text, but only these five are named.

It is not my intention to delve into this interesting aspect of the genealogy in much detail, as it has been the subject of many books and articles, but it is important to briefly remind ourselves of what we know from the Biblical texts about these women.

We read about Tamar in Genesis 38. She marries Er, who according to the text is killed by God for being evil. She then enters into a relationship with the brother of the deceased, Onan, who is instructed to provide her with children, as was the custom in those times. But as it states in verse 9 of this chapter, Onan does not want children by her: 'But since Onan knew that the offspring would not be his, he spilled his semen on the ground whenever he went in to his brother's wife, so that he would not give offspring to his brother'. This angers God, and he 'puts him to death also' (verse 10).

She is then instructed by Judah (her father in law) to remain a widow until his son Shelah grows up. But years later she covers herself, and goes out to find her father in law who is sheering his sheep. Believing her to be a prostitute, he sleeps with her in exchange for his signet, cord and staff and a goat (verses 18 and 19).

When Judah finds out, he commands that she be burnt for her act of whoredom. But Judah defends her: 'Then Judah acknowledged them and said, "she is more in the right that I, since I did not give her my son Selah". And he did not lie with her again'. She goes on to have twin boys. Perez and Zerah.

There is tragedy in Tamar's story: her two husbands are 'killed by God', and Shelah, who is promised to her by her father in law once he is of age, never arrives on the scene. Not only is she widowed, but childless, which at that time would have placed here with the lowest of the low in society, as it was considered a disgrace to be childless. She also would have had no inheritance or means of supporting herself in her old age.

She tricks her father in law into sleeping with her, thereby overcoming the stigma of remaining childless, but also persuades him to give her the symbols of status and wealth: his signet, cord and staff (in addition to the goat he promises her). By taking his signet, staff and cord, she is able to avoid being burned alive, because she can prove who the father of her children would be, and thus ensure that the family line of Judah continued.

According to the gospel of Matthew, Jesus is a descendent of hers, coming through the line of Perez.

Tamar is depicted as wilful and with a mind of her own and able to re-instate herself into the society of the day through her actions. She does not accept that she will remain childless, does not remain passive, but takes action that not only secures her status, but also has the guarantee of the father's symbols of authority and position. Whatever we may think of Tamar, it is interesting that she is included in Jesus' genealogy in Matthew 1. Having already suffered tragedy she is condemned to death, although goes on to bear children after her father in law intervenes on her behalf.

It is not necessary to recount the story of Rahab as it is well known, and narrated in Joshua 2. She is a prostitute who shows great faith and courage, and hides the spies in her house. Her actions protect her and her family, and later ensure that the Canaanites (arch-enemies of the children of Israel) are given some protection. Although there is some dispute as to whether the Rahab mentioned in Mathew's genealogy is the same women depicted in Joshua 2, I see no strong evidence to suggest otherwise. Also: there is an emerging theme in that Tamar and Rahab are associated with prostitution. There is something deeply moving and of real beauty that prostitutes are dignified in this way. They are not objectified, but are shown to have an active role to play in God's plan. This dignifies them, and calls us to always look upon those whom society casts-out with dignity.

The third woman mentioned in Jesus' genealogy is Ruth, the great grandmother of King David. The story of Ruth is well known, featuring as it does in its own right as a short book within the Old Testament canon. Much has been made of her meekness and loyalty, and she has been used by many as role model for humility and honour. Whilst all of this is to be applauded, Ruth's place within Jesus' genealogy is interesting at another level.

Ruth is a Moabite who is accepted into the faith and kinship of the children of Israel. This is significant, because we know from Genesis 19:37 that Moab was one of the sons of Lot, born from the incestuous relationship with his daughter. So the Moabites (who lived in the Transjordan) were often at war with the children of Israel, and practised a polytheistic religion which included human sacrifice.

That Ruth is the great grandmother of King David, and in the ancestry of Jesus, is a reminder of the command which was often not heeded (and certainly not by King David) recorded in Leviticus 19:34: 'The alien who resides with you shall be to you as the citizen among you; you shall love the alien as yourself, for you were aliens in the land of Egypt: I am The Lord your God'.

Bathsheba is also mentioned in Matthew's genealogy, although not by name. She features in verse 6 as 'the wife of Uriah'. She becomes Queen of Israel, wife of David and mother of Solomon. The story is well known: David longs after her as he sees her bathing on a rooftop, and sleeps with her. He then orders for her husband to be sent to the front line in order that he be killed, which is what happens.

The fifth woman to be mentioned in Jesus' genealogy is his mother Mary, a teenager from Galilee who is revered for placing herself in the service of God.

I can hear my feminist friends ask how does this brief reminder of Jesus' genealogy contribute to a positive model of womanhood? After all: three of the five are associated with prostitution and illicit sexual encounters (Tamar, Rahab and Bathsheba) and the remaining two with being humble servants of God (Ruth and Mary). Is this not part of the problem down the centuries, that the role of women has been that of providing sexual pleasure for men, childbirth and being subservient?

There is no question that this has been the case throughout human history, and the Bible, which reflects the times in which it was written is no exception to this. But at the same time, four of the five women mentioned above show real agency. They are not just passive by-standers, but take active roles, are given a voice of their own, and transcend the cruelties and injustices of their particular contexts to shape events around them.

At another level, their place in Jesus' genealogy places inclusivity at the heart of the gospel, and militates against the fanciful ideas of the Immaculate Conception (which states that Mary was never affected by original sin, and her immaculate body was translated directly into heaven without going through death). The doctrine of the Immaculate Conception is pure Platonism, for it claims that perfection pertains to the heavenly realm. It idealises that which is disembodied.

Christ's physical body, flesh and blood, counteracts the platonic obsession with disembodiment. It reminds us that the physical is sacred, for it bears the image of God.

The Bible cannot be detached from the times in which it was written, to read it otherwise devalues it as a series of texts born amidst the struggles of history. It is an account of how different people through the ages have understood God. But it is more than this, because it is also a means by which God communicates to her creation, because she is in the process, always calling (in the still small voice) her people to justice, charity, grace and love. This call at times finds competing with other voices which claim to know exactly what God is saying and demanding, and all is included and presented to us in the biblical texts, with little commentary or help in how to process it all. The Spirit gives life and enables us to read the biblical text and for it to come alive, and shape us and our world. But reading the Bible is a site of struggle, in that struggle we come to engage with God, just as Jacob wrestled with the Angel, and our own autonomy is always wounded and weakened because of it. Our strength as autonomous individuals is broken down, as we limp wounded by the impact of its full effects. But although wounded, we are blessed and in a better place, for we have been offered a vista into the divine, which holds our existence and lives together for the who have eyes to see, for those who are prepared to get wounded.

When you are wounded you recognise the limitations in your own strength...and as the gospel narrative shows, God is not exempt from being wounded.

Women, through the centuries have been wounded through crushing patriarchal systems of control, through binding customs, through exclusion, language, ideology, religion, through sexual intercourse, child birth.

History is written in blood and tears, where the battle between those lusting after dominance and power has trampled and crushed the weak. Men of course, have been victims of this too, and so has God, who ultimately associates with the weak, the poor, the outcast, the down trodden, the accused, the tortured and the crucified.

God too, throughout the Biblical texts, is excluded and misrepresented through language (just as women have been for most of human history). When God has been depicted as a violent warrior-God and ethnic cleanser, his name has been derided and confused with other pagan gods. But for those with ears to hear and eyes to see, amongst the morass of confusing and conflicting images and words, there is a 'still small' voice that is always calling us beyond the blind-spots of our own misconceptions...a weak voice that in the midst of violence and domination calls for us to love and welcome the stranger, a weak voice that speaks through the prophets calling us to social justice. In its weakness there is liberatory power, for it is the voice that sets the captives free and carries us from Exodus and sustains us through exile.

The Bible has been seen as a series of texts that have demeaned and misrepresented women. And yet there is a sense in which God too has been misrepresented too. The Bible presents us with both the moments of misrepresentation and the moments of real epiphany and revelation. This is not about cutting and pasting the verses we like out of the mix according to our 21st century sensibilities, for the beauty and liberatory aspects of the text are interwoven with misconception and human distortions of God. It is all in the mix together, and needs to read as such.

There is always the danger that feminism will replace patriarchy with a mirror image of its angry and controlling self: i.e. that feminism will be little more than an angry mirror image of patriarchy, violence and empowerment for its own sake. A feminism that simply seeks the well-being and promotion of the western elite rather than challenge the structural inequalities of women crushed by structural poverty and power imbalances that confine them to grinding poverty, will do nothing of lasting worth.

We do not need a First World angry feminism that is made in the image of patriarchy. It would be little better, just an inverted mirror image.

What we need is an egalitarian and compassionate re-imagining of gender relations, whereby true masculinity and feminity are dominated by compassion and solidarity. As Henri Nouwen says:

The compassion Jesus offers challenges us to give up our fearful clinging and to enter with him into the fearless life of God himself [...] Through union with him, we are lifted out from our competitiveness with each other into the divine wholeness. By sharing in the wholeness of the one in whom no competition exists, we can enter into new, compassionate relationships with each other. By accepting our identities from the one who is the giver of life, we can be with each other without distance or fear. This new identity free from greed and desire for power, allows us to enter so fully and unconditionally into the sufferings of others that it becomes possible for us to heal the sick and call the dead to life. When we share in God's compassion, a whole new way of living opens itself to us, a way of living we glimpse in the lives of the apostles and this great Christians who have witnessed for Christ through the centuries.[80]

---

[80] Henri J.M. Nouwen, *Compassion: A Reflection on Christian Life* (London & New York: Doubleday, 1983), 20-2.

Chapter 7

Prophet God

This chapter looks at the idea of God communicating through prophets and the prophetic. Prophets are not afraid to speak out in denunciation of structural injustice. The church is called to be a prophetic voice in the world, speaking out against injustice and that which dehumanises individuals and society.

Every generation has its' prophets. Every age has its' prophets. There is something deeply embedded within the human condition that wants change, that wants to listen out for new voices and ideas which challenge existing patterns of thought, existing ways of seeing and understanding the world. Voices that challenge the structures of injustice or mind-sets that keep us prisoners. Voices, like those of good poets, who cause to look at the world in a different way, who challenge our preconceived ideas about what surrounds us, and cause us to see things in a different light. It was the Russian formalist Boris Tomashevsky who was one of the first to coin the word 'defamiliarisation', which was essentially to do with what poetic language and literature do. It should make us see the world in a different way:

> Consider the device of *defamiliarisation* to be a special instance of artistic motivation [..] The old and habitual must be spoken of as it were new and unusual. One must speak of the ordinary as if it were unfamiliar.[81]

---

[81] Boris Tomashevsky, 'Thematics', in *Russian Formalist Criticism: Four Essays*, 2nd edition. Translated with an introduction by Lee T. Lemon & Marion J. Reis. New introduction by Gary Saul Morson (Nebraska: Nebraska U.P., 2012), 66-95 (p.85).

He belonged to a group of thinkers who were questioning everything in the wake of World War I. The War of 1914-1918 with its colossal waste of human life and devastation of Europe and beyond, was not only a human tragedy the scale of which had not been seen before, but also a huge absurd folly. For it was a war that was basically about maintaining the structures of 19th century competing empires, a war to preserve the socio-economic-political structures which had served the modern nation-states well. Of course, nation-states are not homogenised people groups, because the rich always benefit at the expense of the poor and down-trodden. And the Russian Revolution of 1917 in part was brought about by the thousands of conscripts who had seen their fellow soldiers dying in the trenches of the Eastern Front, witnessing first-hand the absurdity and mindlessness of the toll in human lives and misery, being inflicted by so-called advanced nations on one another. Nations with traditions of art and philosophy, nations with developed systems of parliamentary democracy. So-called 'Christian nations' at war with each other. The revolutionaries of 1917 were in part driven by the growing realisation that they had been conscripted to fight in a war to preserve a social order which had excluded the well-being of the masses. They were fighting and dying to preserve a world order which was maintaining the oligarchical structures of power and wealth. And so they decided to revolt. It is in this post 1917 Russia that Tomashevsky and the Russian formalists emerged. In this period of profound questioning of everything which had gone before. They came to understand the power of poetic language to disrupt, upset and reconfigure the way in which we see the world. Words and language had become clichéd through repetitive over use. Like stones in a river which through the perennial flow of water had become rounded, words had become deadened under the weight of cliché. The poets' duty was to 'defamiliarise' that language, to make it strange again. To cause us to see it in a new light. It was as if the poet would pick up one of the rounded stones from the river and hold it up, and show it to us in a different light, revealing a facet to us which had perhaps been hidden until now. This is what good poetry should do. Think about how T. S. Eliot captures the *zeitgeist* of the era with his experimental poem *The Wasteland*, where he writes about 'a heap of broken images, where the sun beats'. Leading up to and afterwards he constructs a landscape which comes alive in new poetic intensity and beauty, causing us to look at the world through different eyes. A poetry born from the chaos and rubble of World War I, expressed in fragmented and difficult lines, and yet no less powerful in its ability to arrest us, to grab our attention and transport us into a poetic world of shifting, ponderous images:

> What are the roots that clutch, what branches grow
> Out of this stony rubbish? Son of man,
> You cannot say, or guess, for you know only
> A heap of broken images, where the sun beats,
> And the dead tree gives no shelter, the cricket no relief,
> And the dry stone no sound or water. Only
> There is shadow under this red rock.
> (Come in under the shadow of this red rock).
> And I will show you something different from either
> Your shadow at morning striding behind you
> Or your shadow at evening rising to meet you;
> I will show you fear in a handful of dust.[82]

---

[82] Extract from 'The Burial of the Dead', *The Waste Land*, by T.S Eliot, *The Norton Anthology of Modern Poetry*, 2nd edition, edited by Richard Ellmann and Robert O'Clair (New York & London: W.W.Norton &Company, 1988), 492.

Prophet God

T.S. Eliot recreates a landscape of 'broken images', borne from a world which has been torn apart. But despite the confusion and decay, it is not without hope, for there is a poetic voice that still calls. Invites. Summons. Calling for us to take shelter under 'the shadow of this red rock'. In T.S. Eliot's poetry the world has been fragmented and destroyed, but re-creation and resurrection are always possible, just like the poetic language of his poetry reimagines, recreates and re conceptualises the world. This is what good poetry should do.

Of course poets and prophets are not synonymous, but there can be considerable overlap, as both can be voices that question and call us to see our world in a different way. Both can call us to open our ears to hear a different tune, which at times can be lost under the clamour of confusing voices that crowd out our thought-life and vie for our attention. Both can subvert from within, and denounce from without.

In Bob Dylan's classic 1964 hit *The times they are a-changing* one of the lines he sings reads 'come writers and critics who prophecy with your pen, and keep your eyes wide, the chance won't come again.' It reminds us of the power of writing to challenge, to question. To build-up and tear down. To give voice to certain feelings, thoughts and images. To silence. Every generation has its poets/prophets, who call us to re-examine ourselves, to question why we believe what we believe, who critique us and our world, in the hope of bringing about personal and structural change for the benefit of society as a whole.

Jewish theologian and scholar Abraham J. Heschel reminds us that 'The significance of Israel's prophets lies not only in what they said but also in what they were [...] The prophet is a person not a microphone'.[83] What Heschel is saying is that words and message which they bring from God is inevitably shaped by both who they are as individuals, and the context in which they were living. This is essential to understand, if we are not to fall into the trap of deploying decontextualised Old Testament prophecy. This can be done without any recourse to the context in which it was written, to justify an image of God that is vengeful and ready to inflict huge suffering on his people when they depart from his ways. I have been in church services where this has been conveyed, backed up by reading isolated verses plucked from the Old Testament prophets.

Heschel restores some balance, looking at prophecy from a holistic viewpoint, reminding us of the pattern of it, and the way in which (in most instances) hope and reconciliation have the final word. Referring to the Old Testament prophets he writes:

> In probing their consciousness we are not interested only in the inward life, in emotion and reflection as such. We are interested in restoring the works of the prophets: terrifying in its absurdity and defiance of its Maker, tottering at the brink of disaster, with the voice of God imploring man to turn to Him. It is not a world devoid of meaning that evokes the prophet's consternation, but a world deaf to meaning. And yet the consternation is but a prelude. He always begins with a message of doom and concludes with a message of hope and redemption. Does this mean that his stillness is stronger that the turmoil of human crimes, that his desire for peace is stronger than man's passion for violence?[84]

Heschel warns against using prophecy as a timeless essence that floats above history and context, which can be re-appropriated *Deus ex machina* anytime we like. Instead, he advocates an understanding of prophecy that is deeply

---

[83] Abraham Heschel, *The Prophets* (New York and Evanston: Harper &Row, 1962), xiii-xiv.
[84] Heschel, *The Prophets*, xiii

contextual. This does not mean that the prophecy cannot project out universal truths, but always from within the vantage point of context:

Prophecy is not simply the application of timeless standards to particular human situations, but rather an interpretation of a particular moment in history, a divine understanding of a human situation. Prophecy, then, may be described as *exegesis of existence from divine perspective*. Understanding prophecy is an understanding of an understanding rather than an understanding of knowledge; it is exegesis of exegesis. It involves sharing the perspective from which the original understanding is done.[85]

The whole issue of how God speaks and reveals herself in the Judaic tradition, through law, the prophets, wisdom literature, theological history, is essential to their spirituality. God, who resides in the cloud of unknowing, and yet who also reveals herself in the cloud, is the prophet-God. Not speaking through natural disasters, but in that 'still small voice', or 'low whisper' as some translations state:

And he said, 'Go out and stand on the mount before the LORD.' And behold, the LORD passed by, and a great and strong wind tore the mountains and broke in pieces the rocks before the LORD, but the LORD was not in the wind. And after the wind an earthquake, but the LORD was not in the earthquake. And after the earthquake a fire, but the LORD was not in the fire. And after the fire the sound of a low whisper. (1 Kings 19:11-12)

That voice which is working through history, calling it deeper. Taking us to its boundaries and limits, away from the centres of power which we set up, to establish a kingdom of the marginalised and those whom the world casts aside. Is this not what is meant by Hebrews 11:32-38:

---

[85]Heschel, *The Prophets*, xvii

And what more shall I say? For time would fail me to tell of Gideon, Barak, Samson, Jephthah, of David and Samuel and the prophets— who through faith conquered kingdoms, enforced justice, obtained promises, stopped the mouths of lions, unquenched the power of fire, escaped the edge of the sword, were made strong out of weakness, became mighty in war, put foreign armies to flight. Women received back their dead by resurrection. Some were tortured, refusing to accept release, so that they might rise again to a better life. Others suffered mocking and flogging, and even chains and imprisonment. They were stoned, they were sawn in two, they were killed with the sword. They went about in skins of sheep and goats, destitute, afflicted, mistreated—of whom the world was not worthy—wandering about in deserts and mountains, and in dens and caves of the earth.

The prophet-God is never silent, even though at times it may seem that way. The eyes of faith enable us to see her at work, and to hear her voice, even through the darkness of history. That voice which calls us to love our enemies, to forgive, to seek for reconciliation, to question and denounce the systems of injustice and corporate greed that shackle the poor and condemn them to lives of privation with no access to adequate resources. That voice which gives voice to the voiceless, which dignifies those on the margins. That voice which speaks to the disfigured and the mentally handicapped and dignifies them because they are made in the image of God. The voice that beautifies and restores the image of love in the created order. It is a 'still small voice' that can barely be heard amongst the cacophony of other voices, but which is there for those who have eyes to see and ears to hear. It is a voice that always calls us deeper, that calls us to question and not accept things at face value, but to try and understand the motives and structures behind everyday life .And it is a voice that always calls us to prayer. Prayers mingled with tears, crying out for love to prevail, for reconciliation and hope amidst the despair and hopelessness of conflict and dehumanisation.

Prayer changes us and our world. Prayer as thanksgiving. Prayer as protest. Prayer as adoration, invocation, intercession. Prayer that instils a different narrative into our lives and our world, because prayer always sees life in terms of gift. Prayer always breaks down the coldness of heart, and makes room for transformative love, for our neighbour, and even our enemy. Prayer changes the way in which we view our world, how we treat the other. It is impossible to dehumanise and inflict violence on those we pray for. You cannot pray for someone, and then see them as inferior to yourself, for true prayer always humbles the heart. True prayer always breaks down the hard shell of prejudices and fears which are such a part of our human condition. And you cannot pray for someone (even your most vilified enemy) and then go on to kill him.

Christ's prophetic command to 'love our enemies' and to do good to those who revile us; have been largely ignored by the Christian world. The speed with which we feel justified to attack and bring down our enemies, should cause us to pause and question if we can really call ourselves Christians. Why is it that issues such as same sex marriage and gender (in)equality are the issues which are splitting the church and the subject of so much discussion? Whilst the majority of the church will happily support those who wage war on our enemies? Have we departed from the central premises of our faith, as recorded on The Sermon on the Mount? How can the church regain its prophetic voice, when it so readily justifies violence?

If we followed Christ's command and example to love our enemies and pray for those who wrong us, our world would be changed. But we don't really read these verses and take them to heart.

A prophetic church is a church which calls us back to prayer.

And we are called to be those who embody that prophetic voice in our world today. To do so, we need ears to hear and eyes to see. We need to listen to the voice of God, who proclaims a different narrative over us. To hear that 'still small voice' amongst the clamour of a thousand voices which bombard us on a daily basis from within and without. The voices of our consumerist late capitalist systems which value us on the basis of our ability to consume, the voices from the beauty pageants and cosmetics industry which value us because of youth and bodily perfection, the voices of secular atheism which switch themselves off to the transformative possibility of the transcendent, and the voices which crush all creativity and which block out the poetic, by imposing monochromatic uniformity on the world.

There is a voice that cries out in the wilderness, outside the circles of earthly power and consumption. That voice still calls us today. Calling us back. Calling us deeper. Calling us further.

Given that this chapter is about prophecy, it makes sense to look in a little more detail and some of the prophetic writings in the Bible. A look at all of them would run into many volumes, so I will briefly reference Amos. The book of Amos is unparalleled in other extant ancient literatures. For it demands justice for the poor and the oppressed. It does not depict them as having deserved their lot, but critiques structural greed and avarice, which drives Yahweh mad with anger.

Just by means of contextualisation, let us remind ourselves of when the major prophetic voices were living. Isaiah was a prophet in the 8th century BC when the children of Israel were under threat from Assyria. Amos prophesied around 750 BC during a period of relative peace and prosperity. Jeremiah prophesied in 6th century BC when there was a threat from Babylon. Ezekiel from prophesies during exile, after fall of Jerusalem in 587 BC.

Amos was prophesying at a time of relative prosperity, but the benefits were being enjoyed by only a small section of society. It is this socio-economic injustice that gives rise to Amos's (and to some extent) Hosea's denunciation of the societies in which they were living. It is interesting that some of the harshest voices of prophetic judgement arose during times of prosperity, rather than in times of oppression. And it is quite clear that the God of the Exodus, the God who had established a covenant with a group of freed slaves, would take social justice seriously.

Chapters 1 and 2 of Amos voice judgement on the other nations, mainly over the issue of how they treated the poor: Amos 2:6 reads 'I will not turn away punishment because they sell the righteous for silver and the poor for a pair of sandals'. In chapter 3 judgement is pronounced on the house of Israel, because they too have neglected the most needy. Chapter 4 denounces (look at verse 1) those who 'oppress the poor and who crush the needy'.

And the prophetic command and call in chapter 5 rings out loud and clear: verses 14 and 15 'seek good and not evil, that you may live, so that the Lord of hosts will be with you .... Hate evil, love good, establish justice in the gate'.

But let us not shy away from the difficult passages, for in that same chapter 5 verses 18 and 19 depict the day of the Lord as pure terror: verse 18 reads 'woe to you who desire the day of the Lord! For what good is the day of the Lord to you? It will be as darkness not light, it will be as though a man fled from a lion and a bear met him, or as though he went into the house, leaned his hand on the wall and a serpent bit him'.

But then, after this passage of woe, in the very same chapter we read the words which were immortalised by Martin Luther King in his speech that changed the course of history when he quoted Amos 5:24 which reads 'But let justice run down like water, and righteousness like a mighty stream.'

What are we to make of this pattern of woe and destruction prophesied which is then followed by an appeal to do justice?

How do we deal with passages such as Amos Chapter 9 where God is depicted as saying (see verse 1) 'I will slay the last of them with the sword' and then later in verse 4 where it reads 'I will set my eyes on them for harm and not for good'.

How do we read into this pattern of violent judgement, apparently commanded by God, without coming to the conclusion that the God we worship is no different to other deities who were set on violence and revenge?

Before I attempt to address that, let me quote from Rabbi Jonathan Sacks:

Every religion based on a body of holy writings, a sacred scripture, contains *hard texts:* passages which, if taken literally and applied directly would lead to results at odds with that religion's deepest moral convictions. There are passages in the Hebrew Bible, the New Testament and the Koran that, taken in isolation, are radically inconsistent with the larger commitments of Judaism, Christianity and Islam to the sanctity of life and the dignity of all persons as bearers of God's image. Such texts need interpretation. The classic form of fundamentalism is belief in the literal meaning of texts, specifically that we can move from the text to application without interpretation. We cannot. Interpretation is as fundamental to any text-based religion as is the original act of revelation itself. No word, especially the word of god, is self-explanatory. Exegetes and commentators are to religion what judges are to law. They are essential to the system, and they can make all the difference between justice and injustice, right and wrong.[86]

So what are we to do with these difficult passages?

At one level, what this pattern of woe and restoration prophesied by the prophets shows, is a growing sense of ethical responsibility and awareness in the society at that time. It shows this, because it paints a picture where human beings are made to take responsibility for their actions, and that their choices have consequences for good or bad.

Made in the image of God, we are dignified by having free wills and the ability to choose.

My free will has direct consequences for those around me for good or for evil, because we live in community.

The depiction of God venting his anger at their behaviour, the passages which talk about natural disasters occurring because of their sin, militates against the blind deterministic world views of other religions and world views of that age.

Part of what is at play in these prophetic texts is an empowering of the human condition: basically a dignifying of the human condition, which made in the image of God, has the ability to affect and bring about change. This is a

---

[86] Sacks, *The Great Partnership*, 251-2.

very different world view from the intractable locked-in structures of Greek mythology, where characters are provided with determined fixed roles which they act out on the stage of life. Not so in the Hebrew Scriptures, where human beings are afforded the dignity of choice and the responsibility that carries. And in the Hebrew Scriptures love and dignity will have the final word. Repeatedly, God breaks into this cycle with justice and mercy.

We must also remember, as theologian Susan McGarry has argued, that the authors behind these prophetic texts were concerned to bring about behavioural reform, and therefore would have been well served by depicting a God of wrath. Ultimately, God's ideal is that we are motivated through love. Whilst the prophetic oracles encouraged ethical accountability and taking responsibility for ones actions, when Christ comes, it is to reaffirm and consolidate God's purpose that we would be inspired and drawn through love.

What are the lessons for us today? We understand God's judgement in different ways from within our world-view and place in history perhaps to what they did then. Very few of us, for example, would interpret weather patterns as expressing Gods judgement, be it Hurricane Katrina or the Indonesian Tsunami in 2004.

What is the application of Amos for us today? Does our relative wealth and materialism in the west lead to fulfilment? Or emptiness? Recent studies have shown that those who are richest in society are not the most happy. There is a pervasive emptiness which can take root, mentioned in Revelation: 'although you think you are rich you have nothing'. Can this emptiness be understood as some form of judgment? As we amass wealth and consume much more of the planet's resources than we should whilst two thirds of the globe live in poverty, is God's wrath heavy on us?

When we live only in reference to our own needs, and when we do not see the pain and suffering of others, both within our own community and further a-field, we distance ourselves from the shalom of God's presence. Instead of union with him, we are left to live out the consequences of our own selfish actions that put our needs first. And even though we think we are rich, we have nothing.

Amos is concerned with the effects of their actions, especially on the poor. He does not pull his punches. And God, who has chosen to bring his kingdom about through us, is angered when our lives and society crush and exclude the most vulnerable. Instead of being instruments of his peace and love, and custodians of his grace and mercy, we can turn in upon ourselves, and experience the emptiness of lives which are not lived in reference to the needs of others, but only to our own. The judgement is that we can remain there, and therefore miss the calling that God has on us to be his hands and feet to a hurting world. How should this shape us? What is the prophetic voice of the church today in terms of the structures of injustice, both global and yet, if we are honest with ourselves, the seeds of which we find in our own hearts?

In the days of Amos they lived with the tensions of hope and despair. When disasters happened, they saw it as God's punishment, when good times came, they saw it as God's blessing. As we confront times of hope and despair, can we see God in it all? As we look out onto the troubles of our world and our communities, can we, through the eyes of faith, still see God at work?

The denunciation of injustice and the defence of the poor in the book of Amos is nothing short of revolutionary given the times it was written in. There is nothing like it in Babylonian, Assyrian or Greek mythology. In most of those religious world views, the poor deserved their lot.

We can still see this kind of religion in practice today. You only have to go to India and witness the horrors of the caste system, where the untouchables are condemned to their poverty because they deserve it by virtue of their class, and how within Hinduism those who are disabled or poor deserve it because they have done something wrong in a previous life.

Not so with Yahweh, who comes in and smashes the systems of oppression, to bring relief and dignity to the captive, and justice and restoration to all.

Karen Armstrong argues:

Amos was the first of the prophets to emphasise the importance of social justice and compassion. In Amos's oracles, Yahweh is speaking on behalf of the oppressed, giving voice to the voiceless... In the very first line of his prophecy as it has come down to us, Yahweh is roaring with horror from his temple in Jerusalem as he contemplated the misery in all the countries of the near East, including Judah and Israel. The people of Israel are just as bad as the Gentiles: they might be able to ignore the cruelty and oppression of the poor but Yahweh could not.[87]

Unlike the deterministic world views of other religions and mythologies of the time, God's restorative and loving action has the final word in the book of Amos, and it will have the final word in our world, where the kingdoms of this world will become the kingdoms of our God, as our hearts are transformed by his grace to ones where we are moved to compassion by the pain and suffering of others.

---

[87] Armstrong, *A History of God*, 58.

At the end of Amos chapter 9, we are given a picture of complete restoration: 'I will bring back the captives of my people Israel, they shall build the waste cities and inhabit them, the shall plant vineyards and drink wine from them, they shall make gardens and eat fruit from them, I will plant them in their land, and no longer shall they be pulled up from the land I have given them, says The Lord your god'.

This is the promise we hold onto. This is the promise we are called to enact. It is little wonder that Martin Luther King quoted the book of Amos. It is little wonder that it became one of the key texts of the Liberation theologians. I would like to end with a quote by Oscar Romero, from his book *Voice of the voiceless*, who was shot when conducting mass for his denunciation of the military leaders of El Salvador. It reads:

The church, like Jesus, has to go on denouncing sin in our own day. It has to denounce the selfishness that is hidden in everyone's heart, the sin that dehumanises persons, destroys families, and turns money, possessions, profit and power into the ultimate ends for which people strive [...] the church has also to denounce what has rightly been called 'structural sin', those social, economic, cultural, and political structures that effectively drive the majority of our people into the margins of society. When the church hears the cry of the oppressed it cannot but denounce the social structures that give rise to and perpetuate the misery from which the cry arises. But also like Christ, this denunciation by the church is not inspired by hatred or resentment. It looks to the conversion of heart of all men and women to their salvation.[88]

---

[88] Oscar Romero, *Voice of the Voiceless: The Four Pastoral Letters and Other Statements*, introductory essays by Ignacio Martin-Baro and Jon Sobrino, translated by Michael J. Walsh (New York, Maryknoll: Orbis Books, 1985), 74.

In the summer of 2014 I had the privilege of spending some time in Central America. Whilst in Managua (Nicaragua) I met priests and activists who had been engaged in setting up the so-called 'comunidades de base', which engaged with a radical spirituality linked to social justice. On a six-hour coach ride from Tegucigalpa in Honduras to El Salvador, I happened to be sitting next to Padre Oswaldo, a Carmelite priest based in San Salvador, although with a pastoral remit which extends across many of the trouble spots of Central America. After hearing about the challenges of doing ministry in a context of spiralling violence, he invited me to stay with his fellow priests at their community.

As I shared with them in their daily rhythms of prayer and the Eucharist, and heard their stories of the challenges of doing ministry in contexts of extreme violence, it reminded me of the central mission of the church: to provide a different liturgical rhythm and pattern to life, to offer hope and beauty amidst despair and violence. I remember attending mass with them, and experiencing a sense of real transcendence, as the music of violins and piano filled the church, and as prayers and incense mingled and filled the air with intercessions for all in need of love and grace.

Padre Oswaldo took me to the university where many priests and students lost their lives after a massacre by part of the paramilitary forces back in the 1980s. I was privileged to briefly meet liberation theologian Jon Sobrino who happened to be passing by. We also visited the church where Oscar Romero was gunned down, and the cathedral in the centre of San Salvador where his funeral took place. Those who processed in mourning were shot at indiscriminately by the paramilitary forces. The levels of violence were unspeakable.

We spoke about Romero and others how had lost their lives in the conflict, and I was reminded of the Archbishop's words recorded in his book *Voice of the Voiceless*, which I make no apologies for quoting in full:

The church is persecuted when it is not allowed to proclaim the kingdom of God and all it entails in terms of justice, peace, love, and truth; when it is not allowed to denounce the sin of our land that engulfs people in wretchedness; when the rights of the people of El Salvador are not respected; when the number mounts steadily of those who have disappeared, been killed, or been calumniated.

It is also important to keep in mind that the church is persecuted because it wills to be in truth the church of Christ. The church is respected, praised even granted privileges, so long as it preaches eternal salvation and does not involve itself in the real problems of our world. But if the church is faithful to its mission of denouncing the sin that brings misery to so many, and it proclaims its hope for a more just, humane world, then it is or secured and calumniated, it is branded subversive and communist.

During this time of persecution the church of the archdiocese has never returned evil for evil, it has never called for revenge or hatred. On the contrary, it has called for the conversion of those who persecute it, and, in our country's difficult problems, it has tried always to promote justice and avert worse evils.

The church hopes, with the help of God, to continue to witness with Christian courage in the midst of difficulties. It knows that only by so doing will it win credibility for what it is proclaiming: that it is a church that has taken its place alongside those who suffer. It will not be frightened by the persecution that it undergoes, because persecution is a reaction to the church's fidelity to its divine Founder and to its solidarity with those in most need.[89]

This is what it means to be a prophetic church. A church which is less concerned about preservation rather than giving itself away.

---

[89] Oscar Romero, *Voice of the* Voiceless, 80.

A church which is not silent in the face of evil and injustice, but which provides a voice, a space, where the structural roots of evil can be denounced, both within the human heart, and in our world at large.

The church needs to regain its prophetic voice to this generation.

Chapter 8

Imageo Dei: re-made in God's image.

Everything goes, everything comes back; eternally rolls the wheel of being. Everything dies, everything blossoms again; eternally runs the year of being. Everything breaks, everything is joined anew; eternally the same House of Being is built. Everything parts, everything greets every other thing again; eternally the ring of being remains faithful to itself. In every Now, being begins; round every Here rolls the sphere There. The center is everywhere. Bent is the path of eternity.

(Friedrich Nietzsche)

For now we see through a glass, darkly; but then face to face: now I know in part; but then shall I know even as also I am known. (1 Corinthians 13:12)

By means of conclusion, I will return to where we began. The Bible is a history of how different generations have understood God, and projected images of the Divine borne from real life struggles through the messy process of human history. It does not float above the world in some platonic detached stratosphere, but as a text is deeply incarnational, in that it emerges and arises in the context of lives lived, of empires rising and falling, of war and exile, hope and promise, judgement and blessing. It is literature, but it is more than that, because it was written and complied by hundreds of editors and scribes down the centuries, who were actively engaged in worshiping communities.

The Bible is also the word of God, in that he speaks to us through it. Like Calvin (who generally gets a bad press these days), I too believe in the inspiration of Scripture, not the written text in isolation, but when we approach the text in a context of worship (be it individual or corporate), allowing it to read us as much as we read it, opening ourselves up to the pneumatological stirrings of the Holy Spirit; then it has a power to transform, call into question, denounce, correct, encourage, inspire. The fact that worshiping communities down the centuries and throughout the ages have found its words to be life-changing and both of comfort and fear at times, should cause even the most hardened agnostic to question its possibilities and effects. No matter how much we may love a Shakespearean sonnet or play, or a novel by Tolstoy or Ian McEwan, a short story by Borges or Kafka; what we are dealing with when we engage with the Bible is different. As Karen Armstrong has argued, it was written in the context of spiritual quest and renewal (no matter how wrong some of its authors were about the nature of God), and as such has the power to transform and change us and our world.

But I have found that whilst God is revealed in Scripture, She is also hidden. Like the image that is revealed in the camera obscura, there are times when we have to wait patiently. When we allow ourselves to be transformed by the God of peace, we let go of all the violent images we have of Him. Amidst the darkness of our world, in the shadows of the dark chamber of life, God is revealed.

Discerning where God is amidst the human projections written and spoken down through the ages, is the work of the Spirit. The Spirit always leads us the God revealed in Jesus. The co-suffering God at one with his creation, gently bringing his image to bear on our world, in the midst of darkness.

At times it is easy to forget that his image is being revealed. We witness so much suffering and injustice on a daily basis that can make us doubt his very existence. But faith calls us back. Prayer calls us back to the God of peace who renews us through hope.

I realise that as I come to the end of these pages, I will have alienated many of my friends, both on the conservative evangelical wing of the church (where my roots lie), and my atheist ones too. As a member and practitioner in the Reformed Tradition (Church of Scotland), the call to reform is central to what we believe as a church. We may differ on many issues regarding the interpretation of scripture and theology; but we all believe in the transforming and salvitic power of Christ, the inspiration of Scripture, and our need as human beings of God.

When all is said and done, the reason why I am a Christian, why I cling on to faith in the midst of profound questioning and doubt, is not because of clever arguments, theological traditions, the church or anything else; it essentially comes to experiential faith lived out (imperfectly) through life's ups and downs. Like Jacob wrestling with the Angel, I wrestle with the whole concept of God, what we have pinned on that name, what has been done in that name (both good and bad), and the teachings of Christ which call for a radical turning away from retribution and violence, to embrace the love of our enemies, and deep down, I am inspired. I know that my life is ever-changing because of it, and that my self-seeking, self-aggrandising attitudes are forever challenged when they are brought prayerfully into the light of God. Change is possible, starting with the individual, but leading out and touching our communities and the world at large, with the promise of shalom. And our world needs this more than ever.

Now I see in part. I see through a glass darkly, struggling as I am within the darkened rooms of the camera obscura, in hope and expectation for the full revelation. Living in this tension transforms me, it changes us, and it opens the way for faith, believing where we cannot clearly see the road ahead, trusting even when there are times when God seems silent, distant, removed... And yet I can feel Her love, as a mother who nurtures her child.... *And now these three remain: faith, hope and love. But the greatest of these is love.* (1Corinthians 13:13).

Bibliography

Amichai, Yehuda. 'Auschwitz'. Www.the atlantic.com/past/docs/unbound/petty/anthology/Amichai/auschwit z.htm (accessed 24.9.2015).

Armstrong, Karen. 'The Idea of a Sacred Text', in *Sacred: Books of the Three Faiths: Judaism, Christianity, Islam*, edited by John Reeve. Essays by Karen Armstrong, Everett Fox, F.E. Peters. Catalogue contributions by Colin. F.Baker, Kathleen Doyle, Scot McKendrick, Drew Nersessian and Llana Tahan (London: The British Library, 2007), 14-20.

Armstrong, Karen. *A History of God* (London: Vintage, 1999).

Armstrong, Karen. *The Bible: The Biography* (London: Atlantic Books, 2007).

Barthes, Roland. *Camera Lucida: Reflections on Photography* (London: Vintage Classics, 1993).

Bloom, Harold. *Genius: A Mosaic of One Hundred Exemplary Creative Minds* (London: Fourth Estate, 2002).

Butler, Judith. *Antigone's Claim: Kinship Between Life and Death* (New York: Columbia University Press, 2000).

Camus, Albert. *The Plague.* Translated by Robin Buss with an introduction by Tony Judt (London: Penguin Books, 2001).

Caputo, John. *The Insistence of God: A Theology of Perhaps* (Bloomington &Indianapolis: Indiana U.P., Indiana Series in the Philosophy of Religion, 2013)

Caputo, John. *The Insistence of God: A Theology of Perhaps* (Indiana Series in the Philosophy of Religion. Bloomington & Indianapolis: Indiana University Press, 2013).

Caputo, John. *The Weakness of God: A Theology of the Event* (Bloomington & Indianapolis: Indiana U.P.,Indiana Series in the Philosophy of Religion, 2006).

Chalke, Steve. 'The Bible and Homosexuality: Part One', which can be found at the following web address: **https://www.premierchristianity.com/Featured-Topics/Homosexuality/The-Bible-and-Homosexuality-Part-One**

(accessed 20.9.2016)

Cobb, John B. Jr., & David Ray Griffin. *Process Theology: An. Introductory Exposition* (Philadelphia: The Westminster Press, 1976).

Daly, Mary. *Beyond God the Father: Towards a Philosophy of Women's Liberation* (London: The Women's Press, 1973).

Dawkins, Richard. *The God Delusion* (London: Black Swan, 2006).

De Beausobre, Julia. *The Woman Who Could Not Die* (London: Chatto & Windus, 1938).

De Beauvoir, Simone. *The Second Sex*, translated and edited by H.M. Parshley (London: Everyman's Library, 1993).

Dear, John. *The God of Peace: Toward a Theology of Nonviolence* (Eugene: Wipf and Stock Publishers, 2005).

De Wit, Hans. '"My God", she said, "Ships make me so crazy": Reflections on Empirical Hermeneutics, Interculturality, and Holy Scripture'. Www.Bible4all.org/be stander/documented/ashx?document-if=33 (accessed 24/9/2915).

Eliot, T.S. 'The Burial of the Dead', *The Waste Land*, *The Norton Anthology of Modern Poetry*, 2nd edition, edited by Richard Ellmann and Robert O'Clair (New York & London: W.W.Norton &Company, 1988), 492.
Foster, Peter. 'Cost to US of Iraq and Afghan Wars could hit $6 trillion', *The Telegraph*, (29.3.2013).

[http://www.telegraph.co.uk/news/worldnews/northamerica/USA/99 61877/Cost-to-US-of   -Iraq-and-Afghan-wars-could-hit-6-trillion.html], accessed on (30.1.2015).

Frazer, James G. *The Golden Bough: A Study in Magic and Religion*, edited by Robert Frazer (Oxford: Oxford U.P., 1994).

Girard, Rene. *Violence and the Sacred* (London: The Athlone Press, 1988).

Hassig, Ross. 'El sacrificio y las guerras floridas', *Arqueología Mexicana* Vol XI, no. 63 (2003), 46-51.
Heschel, Abraham. *The Prophets* (New York and Evanston: Harper &Row, 1962).

Homer. *The Iliad* (Ware: Hertfordshire, 1995).
http://news.bbc.co.uk/1/hi/uk/4098172.stm (Accessed on 22.10.2014)
http://www.theguardian.com/culture/2015/feb/01/stephen-fry-god-evil-maniac-irish-tv], accessed 5.2.2015.

Kafka, Franz. 'Before the Law', www.mit.edu/norvinwww/something else/Kafka?html. (Accessed 24.9.2015).

Keller, Cetherine. *On The Mystery: Discerning Divinity in Process* (Minneapolis: Fortress Press, 2008).

Kierkegaard, Soren. *Fear and Trembling*, edited by C. Stephens Evans & Sylvia Walsh. Translated by Sylvia Walsh (Cambridge: Cambridge U.P., 2006).

Lloyd, Michael. *Cafe Theology: Exploring Love, the Universe and Everything* (London: Alpha International, 2005).

MacDonald, Henry. 'Stephen Fry Calls God 'An Evil, Capricious, Monstrous,   Maniac',   (1st   of   February   2015) [http://www.theguardian.com/culture/2015/feb/01/stephen-fry-god-evil-maniac-irish-tv

Nouwen, Henri J.M. *Compassion: A Reflection on Christian Life* (London & New York: Doubleday, 1983).

Radcliffe, Timothy. *Why go to Church: The Drama of the Eucharist* (London & New York: Continuum, 2008).
Rogers, Chris. 'Where Child Sacrifice is a Business', (BBC News Africa, 11th of October 2011). http://www.bbc.co.uk/news/world-Africa-15255357#story_continues_1 (Accessed on 22.10.2014).

Rollins, Peter. *How (Not) To Speak of God* (London: SPCK, 2006).

Romero, Oscar. *Voice of the Voiceless: The Four Pastoral Letters and Other Statements*, introductory essays by Ignacio Martin-Baro and Jon Sobrino, translated by Michael J. Walsh (New York, Maryknoll: Orbis Books, 1985).

Sacks, Jonathan. *The Great Partnership: God, Science and the Search for Meaning* (London: Hodder & Stoughton, 2012).

Sacks, Jonathan. *The Great Partnership: God, Science and the Search for Meaning* (London: Hodder & Stoughton, 2011).

Sartre, Jean Paul. *No Exit* (New York: vintage books, 1955).

Sophocles. *Antigone.* In *The Three Thebian Plays: Antigone, Oedipus the King, Oedipus at Colonus*, translated by Robert Fagles (London: Penguin, 1984), 54-128.

St Augustine. *Book III: On Christian Doctrine*, translated by R.P.H. Green. (Oxford University Press). (www.pericaritatem.com/2008/02/02/St-Augustine-the-principle-of charity. Ex scripture explicanada est.) accessed 24.09.2015.

Suttle. Tim. 'Fleecing the Flock: A Snapshot of America's Richest Pastors' (http://www.patheos.com/blogs/paperbacktheology/2012/01/fleecing-the-flock-a-snapshot-of-americas-richest-pastors.html, *accessed on 30.12.2014*).

Tallis. Raymond. *Aping Mankind: Neuromania, Darwinitis and the Misrepresentation of Humanity* (Durham: Acumen, 2011).

The Gilgamesh Epic. Translated by N.K.Sanders (Hammondsworth: Penguin, 1972) 108-109.

Tomashevsky, Boris. 'Thematics', in *Russian Formalist Criticism: Four Essays*, 2nd edition. Translated with an introduction by Lee T. Lemon & Marion J. Reis. New introduction by Gary Saul Morson (Nebraska: Nebraska U.P., 2012), 66-95.

Trocme, Andre. *Jesus and the Non-Violent Revolution* (New York: Plough Publishing House, 2011).

Wiesel, Elie. *Night,* translated from French by Marion Wiesel (London: Penguin Books, 2006).

Woolf, Virginia. *A Room of One's Own*, edited with and introduction by Morag Shiach (Oxford: Oxford U.P., 1992).

Zimbardo, Phillip. *The Lucifer Effect: How Good People Turn Evil* (London: Rider, 2007).

Zizek, Slavoj. *Event: Philosophy in Transit* (London: Penguin Books, 2014).

22663368R00122

Printed in Great Britain
by Amazon